T0312037

Hong Kong's 2019–2020 Social Unrest

The Trigger, History and Lessons

Hong Kong's 2019–2020 Social Unrest

The Trigger, History and Lessons

Bernard Yeung

Asian Bureau of Finance and Economic Research, Singapore
& National University of Singapore, Singapore

 World Scientific

NEW JERSEY · LONDON · SINGAPORE · BEIJING · SHANGHAI · HONG KONG · TAIPEI · CHENNAI · TOKYO

Published by

World Scientific Publishing Co. Pte. Ltd.

5 Toh Tuck Link, Singapore 596224

USA office: 27 Warren Street, Suite 401-402, Hackensack, NJ 07601

UK office: 57 Shelton Street, Covent Garden, London WC2H 9HE

British Library Cataloguing-in-Publication Data
A catalogue record for this book is available from the British Library.

HONG KONG'S 2019–2020SOCIAL UNREST
The Trigger, History and Lessons

ISBN 978-981-122-629-8 (hardcover)
ISBN 978-981-122-560-4 (paperback)
ISBN 978-981-122-561-1 (ebook for institutions)
ISBN 978-981-122-562-8 (ebook for individuals)

For any available supplementary material, please visit
https://www.worldscientific.com/worldscibooks/10.1142/11975#t=suppl

Typeset by Stallion Press
Email: enquiries@stallionpress.com

Printed in Singapore

Contents

About the Author

Professor Bernard Yeung[1] is Stephen Riady Distinguished Professor in Finance and Strategic Management at the National University of Singapore (NUS) Business School. He is also the President of the Asian Bureau of Finance and Economic Research. He was Dean of NUS Business School from June 2008 to May 2019. Before joining NUS, he was the Abraham Krasnoff Professor in Global Business, Economics, and Management at New York University (NYU) Stern School of Business and the Director of the NYU China House. From 1988 to 1999, he taught at the University of Michigan and at the University of Alberta from 1983 to 1988.

Professor Yeung has published widely in top tier academic journals covering topics in Finance, Economics, and Strategy; his writing also appears in important media publications such as the *People's Daily*, *The Financial Times*, *The Economist*, and *The Wall Street Journal.*

He was awarded the Public Administration Silver Medal (2018) in Singapore, Irwin Outstanding Educator Award (2013) from the Academy of Management and is an elected Fellow of the Academy of International Business.

---

[1] I would like to acknowledge the helpful comments by Aline Wong, Stefano Feltri, and seminar participants at the East Asian Insititute — NUS, Entrepreneurs' Organization Singapore and Entrepreneurs' Organization Hong Kong, Singapore China Friendship Association Women's Alliance Inaugural Lecture, and the Stigler Center at the University of Chicago Booth. All errors are my responsibility.

Professor Yeung was a member of the Economic Strategies Committee in Singapore (2009), a member of the Social Science Research Council (SSRC) in Singapore (2016–2018) and a member of the Financial Research Council of the Monetary Authority of Singapore (2010–2013).

Professor Yeung received his Bachelor of Arts in Economics and Mathematics from the University of Western Ontario, and his MBA and PhD degrees from the Graduate School of Business at the University of Chicago.

Chapter 1

Introduction

I was born and raised in Hong Kong. Like many others, though I have lived abroad for many years, my extended family remains in Hong Kong, the place is my home in my heart and spirit. Hiking on Hong Kong's numerous trails on weekends and seeing the night lights at the Peak, I am still continually charmed by Hong Kong's natural and man-made beauty. The business districts are filled with energy, creativity, and resourcefulness. Hong Kong's transportation infrastructure is world-class and modern: the subway and highway systems connect seamlessly with the century-old peak-tram and electric tramways, moving millions of people around daily. Luxurious hotels and restaurants co-exist with homey noodle shops featuring inexpensive staple wonton noodles. Malls with expensive brand names may be next to simple no-frill bargain shops. They together offer a huge variety of comfortable consumption choices for hardworking people from all walks of life. There is no doubt: Hong Kong is a beautiful, liveable, and vibrant city!

Hong Kong's proud achievements are the results of extreme hard work by multiple generations. They have elevated Hong Kong from a backward fishing village in 1842 to a world-class financial centre in the 21st Century. It ranked 4th in the World Bank's 2018 Human Capital Index and 5th in the Ease of Doing Business Index. Even the Cato Institute, which is critical towards China, reported that Hong Kong's level of Individual Freedom in 2019 was third in the world, behind only New Zealand and Switzerland. Hong Kong's 2019 per capita

GDP was 15th in the world, ahead of Germany, France, and the UK, according to the IMF World Economic Outlook (October 2019).

Sadly, this miraculous Hong Kong had been plagued by social unrest since the middle of 2019. The proposal to amend an existing extradition bill in February 2019[2] triggered a year-long social unrest since June 2019. Many peaceful protests ended in torturous violence. Many ordinarily pragmatic Hong Kongers appeared to be suddenly driven by social media rumours and lost their sanity. Dr. Jekyll of Hong Kong became Mr. Hyde. Protesters, or rioters, blocked highways, destroyed railroads and subway stations, almost dismantled two university campuses, and many shops. They terrorized opposition. They set a disagreeing person on fire (he survived); they threw rocks and killed a person cleaning up debris that protesters had left behind. They claimed police brutality to sustain their protests. Thousands were arrested and nearly a billion dollars of properties were damaged. Mass media around the globe focused on Hong Kong and many openly supported the protest. The people of Hong Kong were incredulous: how were these all happening in their beloved home?

The 2019–2020 social unrest has turned Hong Kong into a deeply fractured society: yellow (anti-government and anti-China) vs. blue (anti-protesters and pro-establishment). The deep yellow believe that they are fighting a "just war". Others in the same camp are sympathetic to the protesters, seeing them as brave youth venting their anger and standing up against an incompetent puppet government and dictators. The blue members see the protesters as rioters naively mesmerised by false prophecies with self-interest. They also view the riots as a "colour revolution" orchestrated and financed by outside forces to sacrifice

---

[2] The existing extradition bill excludes China and territories considered to be a part of China. The proposed amendment allows the HK government to consider requests on extradition of criminal suspects from a government of any location which include Mainland China, Taiwan and Macau. Requests would be decided on a case-by-case basis by the Chief Executive. The HK courts would have the final decision on whether to grant an extradition request. The suspected offence needs to be also considered a crime in Hong Kong. Furthermore, under the bill, Hong Kong would only hand over a fugitive for an offence carrying a maximum sentence of at least seven years.

Hong Kong to drag down China and the Communist Party of China (CPC). They opine that the yellow campers have no right to destroy Hong Kong's prosperity that they did not build. Long-time friends can no longer rationally discuss their differences if they belong to different "colour" camps. Politics is now taboo in family conversations.

Hong Kong is currently experiencing very significant economic hardship, especially amongst the lower-income classes: the social unrest has wiped out the cash reserves of small- and medium-sized enterprises, especially in the F&B, retail, and construction industries; the Covid-19 pandemic is completing the job of sinking Hong Kong's economy. Many globally famous restaurants, e.g., Jimmy's Kitchen, Lin Heung Tea House, and the Jumbo Seafood floating restaurant in Aberdeen are currently closed with uncertain possibility of re-opening. Of course, there have been many lay-offs. Fresh graduates from universities cannot find jobs. The city, overcast by a thick cloud of sadness, uneasily contains a growing mass of jobless and penniless people anxious about their future. Very unfortunately, the middle and lower middle income classes can ill-afford the economic damage.

Despite the widespread economic miseries caused by the unrest and the threatening pandemic, the conflict drags on; small scale activities are re-emerging every now and then. This is because the yellow camp has neither achieved what they want, e.g., to control the government; nor has it encountered any effective deterrence to their actions. Therefore, the Opposition faction is doing what they can to sustain the intense emotions. As such, Hong Kong's governability and its future may be jeopardised.

Here are some illustrative Yellow campers' behaviour. A medical sector workers' union launched a 5-day strike at the beginning of February, seeking to pressure the government to forbid Chinese entry into Hong Kong; their behaviour hinders the city's efforts to battle the pandemic. Some restaurants and salons, citing the threat of Covid-19, have openly declared that they would not accept Mandarin-speaking Chinese customers except those from Taiwan (note that many Mainland Chinese are legitimate long-term Hong Kong residents); thus fostering animosity rather than cooperation.

Politicians backing the Yellow camp used filibusters and other means to stall the Legislative Council's work from Oct 2019 to May 2020. They did that at a time when the Council needed to work on many legislations to tackle deep economic distress and other bills like maternity leaves. The Yellow campers are openly maneuvering to take up as many seats in the Legislative Council in September 2020 election. They claim this is justified in the name of pursuing their vision of the future.

Hong Kong's society is struggling to get rid of a vicious vortex of cynicism, distrust, and discordance. Chinese should remember the Chinese proverb, "A family in harmony prospers, but decline and discordance breed each other".

A Mammoth Task Challenged by Accountability-Light Opposition Politics

Many are shocked and perplexed: what has caused the dramatic and depressing changes in Hong Kong? Some suggest effective external influences. One key belief in Asia is that an intrinsically strong body can resist undesirable extrinsic influences, just like a body with a strong immune system can resist germs and viruses. This book's focus is therefore on Hong Kong's internal issues. The current dismal atmosphere in Hong Kong has been in the making for decades. Multiple factors are rotting Hong Kong's core. Digging into Hong Kong's history, political structure, the evolution of its society, and the challenges stemming from changes in the external environment is a revealing and profound intellectual journey.

In 1997, Hong Kong was returned to China. The ultimate objective is full reintegration with China. This is a daunting task for Hong Kong's government. There is no historical precedent of bringing a tiny modern post-colonial state (a population of 7.5 million) with the rule of law, high level of civil rights, and a fundamentally private-sector-dominant market economy into a huge socialist state (a population of 1,409 million). What would be Hong Kong's path?

In 1997, China the socialist state was struggling to develop a market system. In 2020, it describes itself as being a "socialist market economy" system. China has a formidable and energetic private sector. Still, the state has dominant economic and political powers unmistakably concentrated in the hands of the Communist Party of China. It is my guess that the CPC technocrats in 1997, like many of us, did not have enough knowledge about what Hong Kong's re-integration journey entailed. They could have been hoping to learn from Hong Kong's own "leaders", who were unfortunately as clueless, if not more. Now, China is the second-largest economy in the world (and by purchasing power the largest). China's CPC has become confident of its "socialism with Chinese characteristics."[3]

Hong Kong, like the rest of the world, has had to adjust to China's phenomenal growth in the past twenty years. Credit is due to China for her success. At the same time, under-equipped politicians have unwittingly allowed the benefits of China's rise to accrue to the rich. However, the costs of adjustment fell disproportionately onto the lower-income classes. Hong Kong does have the advantage of being a part of China. Hong Kong politicians have sadly squandered the advantage.

The Basic Law liberates Hong Kong from more than 150 years of colonial authoritarianism at the 1997 handover. It establishes in Hong Kong a democratic balance of power between the Executive Branch and the Legislative Council. However, Hong Kong politicians are inexperienced. At the same time, Hong Kong does not have the socio-ecological system to hold politicians accountable for what they do. To make things worse, Hong Kong has a coalition of opposition holding onto a political ideology not amiable to re-unification even before the 1997 handover to China. A strange type of opposition politics emerges, as we shall describe below and also elaborate on in subsequent chapters.

The conflicting interests of the Executive Branch and the Opposition faction evolved into **an accountability-light political tug of war since the handover,** generating utterly non-coherent policies that haunt the public, raise Hong Kong's costs of living, and hollow out the general

---

[3] See "CPC creates Xi Jinping Thought on Socialism with Chinese Characteristics for a New Era," Source: Xinhua| 2017-10-19 00:28:09|Editor: Hou Qiang.

public's economic opportunities. The accountability-light system allows self-serving Opposition politicians to pursue their self-declared noble goals, which have only, at best, tangential relations with the economic future of Hong Kong. They and their allies push hard on all fronts an anti-CPC blame narrative and nativism in Hong Kong. At the same time, the Executive Branch, in practising its free-market principles, has created a haven for business tycoons.

The result is a factionalised Hong Kong society with a split identity. The older and richer group is fixated on preserving their economic prosperity and bury their heads in their own meritocracy trap in judging the young people. The younger generation is overwhelmed with economic grievances, harbours animosity towards China, and has a sense of hopelessness in its search for identity. Many of them grew up with almost two decades of annual anti-CPC, anti-China, and anti-government rallies. Through these rallies, participants are socialized to believe that CPC is repressively chipping away Hong Kong's democracy and freedom. Their sentiment fuels the 2019–2020 year-long unrest which has brought Hong Kong to its knees.

Important Lessons from Hong Kong

Hong Kong experiences a condensed and intensified version of the consequences of social fractionalisation and identity politics, which many countries, including advanced Western countries, are facing. We should all strive to understand and learn from Hong Kong's experience. Our world is dynamic. In adjusting to changes, multiple income classes and age groups of the current and future generations have conflicting interests. The government and the market have to balance these interests. That can be done only if the society has a common identity and the ability to make informed rational choices based on prudent expectations.

Hong Kong demonstrates many wrong moves. It has created an appearance of success as measured by per capita GDP, the abundance of the rich, and the growth in its financial sector. However, underneath all of these is impotent democracy at its worst. Accountability-light politics allows politicians to thrive on rhetoric and blame narratives instead of attending to fundamentals like education and long-term economic planning. A blame narrative is not based on logic but relies on stirring up emotions and feelings. A blame narrative with a conspiracy hypothesis is particularly appealing to the underprivileged. Hong Kong has established the following formulae: accountability-light politics produces a blame narrative which leads to destructive identity politics and unrest. The result is the tearing apart of national unity as well as fanatic emotions that trump rational thinking. Hong Kong ends up losing its ability to adjust to a changing world while its chaotic politics continues to dim its own future.

One purpose of this book is to reveal Hong Kong's journey as matter-of-factly and as objectively as possible. The book will trace the historical development of Hong Kong's accountability light politics and how for two decades it generates internally inconsistent policies that cause economic grievances. The book also provides historical accounts of annual rallies and the 2019-2020 year-long unrest. It provides analyses of the long process in inducing the younger generation to internalize a blame narrative against China and its government.

Knowledge empowers judgement. The fate of Hong Kong depends on collective prudent judgements. Knowledge is built on critical thinking. Critical thinking entails collating and analysing facts, as well as distilling truth from facts. It also depends on logic auditing of inferences — checking assumptions, causality, and robustness in interpretations. I sincerely hope the Hong Kong society can acquire critical thinking that leads to knowledge, not cynical thinking that breeds destructive behaviour.

The other purpose of this book is to identify for Hong Kong the long-term and short-term solutions. The government has challenging work to do. It needs to rebuild Hong Kong's identity and to raise its level of intelligence, including improving its education and information flow in society. In the short run, it needs to engage all level of Hong Kongers to launch a government-citizen partnership in amending many of the society's shortcomings.

We ought not underestimate Hong Kong's resilience. Hong Kong still has the basics: the rule of law, creativity, and a self-reliant spirit. It has human capital and a great majority wants a peaceful and steady progress. It could still morph from its current situation into a spirited society with a vibrant market guided by a government which respects the rule of law and individualism, yet inside a communist country. It could be a democratic society inside China that combines the best of the East and West. Where there's a will, there's a way. Many around the world want Hong Kong to succeed.

Before turning to the organisation of this book, let us take a snapshot of Hong Kong's historical journey, the details of which are laid out in subsequent chapters.

History I: Early Riots and Recovery

Despite the depressing current situation, we should remain hopeful. Hong Kong had its share of social unrest before. Every time, it bounced back rigorously.

Colonised since 1842, Hong Kong's trading economy attracted Chinese from the Mainland. Hong Kong's early population comprised over ninety percent of Chinese migrants from the Mainland, labelled as colonial subjects. After the establishment of the People's Republic of China in 1949, Hong Kong experienced another influx of poor immigrants from the Mainland. This caused housing shortages and depressed wages, leading to high income disparity. Major riots ensued, in 1956 and 1967, each resulting in more than 50 deaths and thousands arrested. The 1956 unrest was instigated by a flag desecration incident leading to physical conflict between Chinese in Hong Kong supporting the government in Beijing and those supporting the government in Taipei. The 1967 unrest stemmed from a labour dispute in a factory. The basic drivers were fractionalisation of Hong Kong Chinese and built up discontent stemming from poor living conditions and labour standards for the lower-income classes. An illuminating pattern emerged. The British colonial government then did pull out strong measures to stop rioting, to control the mass media, and to forbid anti-subervsion activities.

However, the society also took reconciliatory steps. Fractional groups came to accept their common identity – Chinese in a safe harbour. The government introduced applaudable new policies that encompassed the building of public housing and the passing of a long series of comprehensive reforms which included developing District Councils, the MTR, compulsory education, paid holidays, labour safety requirements, and homeownership schemes.

The cooperation between government and people, as well as Hong Kongers' self-reliant spirit, propelled Hong Kong into the first world after these riots. Hong Kong's amazing rebound from chaos was based on two factors: collective resolve to make Hong Kong work and a reconciliatory government attending to the dissatisfactions and grievances of the underprivileged. These were feasible because Hong Kong residents maintained a common identity (Chinese living in Hong Kong) and because branches of the government were united in focusing on working for the city. We can surely learn from that.

History II: Opposition Politics, Hong Kong Style

Almost two decades of development since 1967 was met with the concern that a part of Kowloon and the New Territories had only been leased to the British government until 1997. The Sino-British Joint Declaration in 1984 committed Britain to duly return Hong Kong to China in 1997 and Beijing to preserve Hong Kong's system and let Hong Kongers run Hong Kong. Many sincerely welcomed the arrangement. The Basic Law, Hong Kong's mini-constitution, was approved by the Standing Committee of the National People's Congress in China in 1990. It stipulates that Hong Kong may preserve its government structure (but elevates the independence and the power of its Legislative Council). It also stipulates that only Hong Kong citizens are allowed to take seats in the Executive and Legislative Branches. It promises Hong Kong's gradual and orderly progress towards universal suffrage in selecting its Chief Executive and Legislative Council members (Article 45); it guarantees Hong Kong freedom of speech and association (Article 27). At the same time, it stipulates that Hong Kong is an inalienable part of China (Article 1) and should not be a base for subversive activities

(Article 23). Article 5 declares that the socialist system and policies shall not be practised in Hong Kong and its capitalist system shall remain unchanged for 50 years from 1997, which may or may not mean that Hong Kong's government system will be fully integrated into China thereafter.

The Basic Law drafting committee formed in 1985 comprised prominent leaders in Hong Kong and members from China. Unfortunately, the crackdown on the June 4th 1989 Tiananmen Square protest created huge distrust of the CPC; some very prominent Hong Kong representatives resigned from the committee. Some of them formed the core political opposition, and later many young people growing up in Hong Kong became their supporters. These core members and their strong supporters have tried since then to attain their preferred changes in Hong Kong, including their only version of universal suffrage (among many other versions), a liberal and unconditioned version of one-person-one-vote.

The political "reforms" led by the British-Hong Kong government in the mid-1980s, intensified by the last British appointed Governor Chris Patten, have long-lasting impacts. Firstly, Chris Patten in 1994, against the advice of experienced British hands, including multiple ex-governors and a highly ranked British foreign policy advisor, changed the formation and memberships of the Legislative Council. China nullified Patten's Legislative Council, claiming that Patten's changes violated the Basic Law. This cemented the development of a core coalition opposing to any pro-China political and policy stances. The coalition has been challenging the Executive Branch's policies and hindering efforts to further integrate Hong Kong into China. Secondly, the British-Hong Kong government liberalised mass media control, unleashing a venue for vociferous opposition, often in a cynical tone. Thirdly, the reforms installed in 1993 a generous welfare program, the *Comprehensive Social Security Assistance*, which attracted many lower-income Chinese immigrants; thereby providing fodder for some Hong Kong residents to developed a negative attitude towards the new migrants from the Mainland. These actions planted the seeds for the social and political discordances that have been affecting Hong Kong since 1997.

The post-1997 governance structure in Hong Kong, comprising the Executive Branch, Legislative Branch, and independent Judiciary, produced two decades of tug of war between the Executive Branch and multiple interest groups. Before 1997, Hong Kong had an apparently similar governance structure but *in reality, it was not so*. During the colonial period, governors were appointed by the British Colonial Foreign Affairs Office or even directly by the Prime Minister. The appointed governor chaired both the Executive Council and the Legislative Council, appointed enough "official" members and held multiple ex-officio votes. Essentially, the England-appointed governor controlled both Councils and he was directly accountable only to the British government. The Basic Law created a political structure that empowers the Legislative Council in the sense that it has ways to get rid of the Chief Executive, e.g., by repeatedly not passing her budget. The Basic Law has created for Hong Kong "opposition politics" that ties the hands of the Executive Branch. Chapter 7 will explain that the Basic Law introduces democracy in Hong Kong.

Generically, after 1997, opposition groups can have multiple means to hinder the passing of legislations even if they do not control the Legislative Council. Their accountability and their real commitments are open questions. Nobody disciplines their self-serving political behaviour. The government has correspondingly failed on many fronts.

For example, due to the Legislative Council's opposition, the Executive Branch failed to raise the minimum residency requirement to qualify for welfare payments. The defeated legislation was intended to reduce the economic attraction and thus slow down the immigration flow. Meanwhile, Hong Kong's free hospital care and right of abode for babies born in Hong Kong attracted a huge influx of expectant mothers from the Mainland to Hong Kong to deliver their babies. The public complained. The Legislative Council did not establish legislation to stop the practice. It took a 2011 public rally to get there. With the help of the "free media", a very negative sentiment developed in Hong Kong towards Mainland Chinese — they were taunted as "locusts" swarming to grab Hong Kong's resources slated for welfare and hospital medical care.

The resultant influx of immigrants stressed the housing situation, among other issues. Yet, the Legislative Council constrained the Executive Branch's ability to allocate resources to build government-sponsored affordable housing. One could speculate that these benefited owners of lower price houses. Developers took the cue, especially after the liberalisation of rent controls in 1998, to pursue monopolistic behaviour in housing.

Furthermore, the surge in land value came just as China started its post-WTO (2001) strong growth. Since then, manufacturing jobs have all but moved to the Mainland while the financial sector has surged. Hong Kong's open market policy in financial and human capital flow (except to the medical sector) has further pushed up real estate prices, aggravated the hollowing out of business opportunities in the middle, and intensified competition for human-capital-intensive jobs. The economic policy would allow Hong Kong and China to develop a mutually beneficial relationship akin to that of Manhattan and the United States. However, the Opposition hindered the progress of this strategy by retarding integration between Hong Kong and China.

A pattern emerged. The Executive Branch inherited the past "free market policy" philosophy catered to unfettered profit-seeking. Hardened opposition always catered to opposing the Executive Branch's policies. Whilst some opposition might be meaningful, the Opposition also resisted any policies that could enhance Hong Kong's integration with China, and had, at times, gone to the extent of opposing key elements in the Basic Law. The Opposition's brand of "convenient populism" left the Hong Kong public with vacillating policy directions harmful to the lower-income group, e.g., shifting from liberal immigration policy to limiting the development of affordable housing, thereby raising their accommodation cost. The Opposition camp also resorted to developing anti-China and nativism movement in multiple fronts, including in the education sector.

Collectively, the Hong Kong government delivered internally inconsistent policies, resulting in huge economic disparity. The policies created uneven distribution of the benefits (to the rich) and costs (to the poor) in their adjustments to global economic changes. Furthermore, the government ill-prepared the younger generations for a rising China.

Unfortunately, the Opposition and their allies continued to ignore the looming economic hardship of ordinary Hong Kongers. The Opposition, the Civil Human Right Front, and some mass media ran a continuous negative campaign against the Executive Branch and the Beijing government. They organised almost annual political rallies since 2003 for universal suffrage, against a national security bill, against government-business cronyism, against mainland Chinese women giving birth in Hong Kong, etc. (Whether China forbids universal suffrage in Hong Kong is debatable, see Instruments 23 and 24 of the Basic Law.) In the discordant atmosphere, the Executive Branch turned increasingly reactive to the antagonistic attitude and ended up losing touch with Hong Kongers.

The Opposition is trapped in their own anti-China narrative because not sustaining the narrative would mean losing their legitimacy. It accordingly pushes relentlessly their anti-China narrative. The Opposition and their allies have succeeded in pounding onto the younger generation the impression that China is "repressive" and Hong Kong is losing its "civil rights and freedom". The Occupying Central movement in 2013 was a prelude. They used the extradition bill to ignite in 2019 the current long-lasting unrest.

Displaying Dissatisfaction

One can be sympathetic to the young people's vociferous complaints. They have no control over Hong Kong's fractionalisation and the resultant inconsistent policies that directly affect them. They feel ignored and helpless. Their destructive actions damage Hong Kong and their own future. The young people, however, passionately and self-righteously view their actions as a revolution: a bid to impose their own rules of the game, including nativism, and to rewrite the social power hierarchy. Their social media groups have been sustaining their emotions and serving as their communication infrastructure in organising and coordinating their activities.

The causes of the younger generation's economic, social, and political stresses deserve careful analyses and constructive remedies. However, the causal connection between the political system in China and the younger generation's economic plight remains very unclear. Unfortunately, the young people's actions, the police attempts to contain them, and the government's long period of inaction have collectively turned Hong Kong into an even more divided society with a very uncertain future. The movement has morphed into an explicitly anti-China-anti-Government campaign, or in the supporters' terms, "revolution", with no constructive and attainable goal. It is sustained by a questionable accusation of police brutality. All these push China's government to find a solution to put a halt to the disruption.

It is very heart-breaking to witness that the movement has gravely damaged Hong Kong's economy and dimmed its future outlook. Even more depressingly, the younger generation will again be the recipients of worsening economic plight in the future. Even after stopping the disruption, taking care of the sizeable portion of lost young people and reintegrating them in a normal Hong Kong will be a daunting challenge.

Accountability-Light Politics

History allows us to trace the development of Hong Kong's accountability-light politics, which develops in Hong Kong at the worst possible time. It is worth explaining further here even though some parts below appear repetitive.

Societies often face dynamic adjustments. Hong Kong has been much affected by the changes in China and changes in China's economic and political relationships with the rest of the world. In the past, Hong Kong endured and survived a worse influx of immigrants, housing shortage, high-income inequality, and rapid changes in industrial composition. People with different ideologies nevertheless banded together because of their common identity (Chinese). When challenged, like in 1956 and 1967, branches of the government delivered reconciliatory remedial policies for they were unified in preserving Hong Kong. The mass media was tame; social media was absent. The system was not perfect but worked: the government was disciplined enough to represent multiple groups and generations, though not necessarily evenly. The Hong Kong magic in the past was that the market, the state, and society had a common identity; they prudently cooperated to overcome adversities and differences.

After 1997, Hong Kong's political fabric and structure changed. Given the Basic Law, the Hong Kong government's mission is to guide Hong Kong into full integration with China. The Hong Kong government comprises the Executive Branch, the Legislative Council, and the Judiciary. They are supposed to form a system with reasonable checks and balances. The precondition for the system to work is that there is sufficient accountability to discipline politicians to collectively serve Hong Kong's people.

Unfortunately, the system delivered accountability-light politics. Accountability-light politics refers to the phenomenon of society not having a sufficiently mature mechanism to hold a politician responsible for the consequence of the policy he/she has advocated. Hong Kong does not have the mechanism because before the 1997 handover of Hong Kong back to China, the city had an authoritarian system since colonisation in 1842. When accountability is lacking, multiple factions of politicians pursue self-interests in shaping Hong Kong's policymaking, which results in harmful, inconsistent, and incoherent policies.

The Executive Branch and the pro-business camp have consistently pursued "pro-market" policies. Rich tycoons are presumably endowed with connections to Beijing and have their interests covered. The Executive Branch caters to delivering the performance indicators they think Beijing sets. Most Hong Kongers would agree on the need for some balance. Yet, the Opposition has not advanced effective policies to improve the lives of the "houseless and low economic opportunity" group. Their political agenda has evolved from embracing immigrants to nativism. This results in hindering progressive policies and ends up inadventently collaborating with the camp they oppose in creating stresses in housing and health care for the majority of Hong Kongers.

The Opposition harbours other wishes, including making their preferred changes in Hong Kong and resisting the application of the Basic

Law. The constant in their behaviour is an anti-establishment, anti-China influence: they build a negative narrative on China and push for an unconditional one-person-one-vote election of the Chief Executive and legislators. Their political behaviour negatively affects Hong Kong's journey in adjusting to the rise of China. These politicians' goals may be noble, at least in their minds, e.g., to keep Hong Kong "free of China" after 2047. However, are these goals consistent with the Basic Law and the Sino-British Joint Declaration in 1984? Are these truly democratic choices, or are they just the Opposition's private objectives? The costs of pursuing their goals fall onto the younger generation and further damage their future outlook.

In the midst of this tug of war, youth in the not well-endowed families face a hollowing out of opportunities. However, as they are growing up, the Opposition and some mass media have been pitching to them the anti-CPC, anti-China, and anti-government blame narrative. As well, they have observed or even participated in many rallies of the same nature. While previous generations of Hong Kongers grew up apolitical but committed to economics and being Chinese, these youth grow up almost excessively political and doubtful of their Chinese identity.

It is very important to recognize that Hong Kong's accountability-light politics shows something puzzling. The Opposition has quite successfully created a blame narrative unfavourable to the government and societies on the Mainland. The accusation (before the protests/riots) that China has been repressive of Hong Kong, eroding Hong Kong government's autonomy, and interfering with the running of Hong Kong's policies does not seem to be based on evidence, as Chapter 6 will explain. However, the selling of the storyline is successful. It has become the adopted stance for many in the younger generation. How is it done? Via the education system? Via the mass media? Via social media? Is there some truth in the narrative? Is narrative politics based on conspiracy theory and confirmation bias so powerful that it trumps facts and truth-seeking from facts? How does the blame narrative affect Hong Kong youth's national identity? Hong Kong's troubles provoke us all to think. We present in depth analyses on these issues: accountability light politics, blame narrative, and the lost of a coherent national identity in Chapters 4, 6, 7 and 8.

One Solution

Hong Kong society today is teeming with dissatisfaction. This is actually a chance to utilise constructive dissatisfaction — to do something positive to improve the situation. Let us appeal to people's good nature. In life, the worst time is the best time for reconciliation and cooperation. All parties, politicians in all camps, police, protesters, civilian groups, the mass media, and many more, should ask themselves whether they have, individually or collectively, contributed to the mayhem due to their decisions and behaviour now or in the past, no matter how noble their original motivation might be. It is time to step back, reflect, drop accusing fingers, and reconcile. This would be a major step toward long-term healing and redevelopment.

The government, the market, and the society can work together to fix Hong Kong's problems — reconstruct a sense of belonging and a coherent Hong Kong identity, establish factual and respectful communication between government and people, strengthen the accountability between politicians and the people they serve, develop affordable housing, increase inclusive growth and vertical mobility, create industrial renewal, ..., the list may be long but can also be energising. Fundamentally, Hong Kongers can re-engineer a new consensus to allow the city to move forward constructively, based on inclusive growth and a balanced and rational approach to resolving social issues. Hong Kong can become a shining example to the world about what an intelligent society with a coherent spirit can do: be our own rational master choosing to do the right thing. The world will applaud.

The situation in Hong Kong is not unique. The world today faces disruptive changes due to globalisation and technological progress, aggravated by the need to accommodate the economic growth of densely populated countries in Asia. As economic disparity grows and anxiety surges, these naturally lead to huge dissatisfaction on many fronts. Opportunistic politicians cultivate nativism and protectionism from the dissatisfaction to achieve their own goals. The prevalence of social media usage and its ability to spread fake news, amplifies emotions which breed misanthropy and allow tribune to trump experts and logic. Can

Hong Kong set itself apart and be different? Can it be a positive example for turning destructive dissatisfaction into constructive reflection and cooperation for a better and more pleasant future?

Democracy and Freedom

Finally, we recognise that "democracy and freedom" is emphasised in Hong Kong's current social unrest. But we must beware that democracy and freedom in form but not in substance only gives us chaos and democracy tax.

Democracy and freedom are not pre-destined to be the prerogative of any system. They are built on a society with a collective identity and intelligence grounded on strong education which emphasises strong moral values. The building of democracy and freedom also requires an intelligent government that cares for the current and future generations of people. The government needs to guide itself, the market, and its voters to make and accept hard policy choices that balance the provision of a safety net, inclusive growth, individual responsibility and interest, and long-term efficiency. The government also needs to continuously cultivate and maintain the development of social values, strong educational institutions, and an informed society with a national identity. Unless embodied within such a society, democracy and freedom are words that exist on vacuous high moral grounds.

Indeed, a democratic and free society is not built overnight. Even the "advanced democracies" that the Western press would consider existing in Britain, Western Europe, and the US took hundreds of painstaking years to build their still imperfect systems which remain fragile. The process includes overcoming wars, blatant discrimination and voting exclusivity, corruption, and scandals. It always involves the collective ability to reflect and correct past mistakes.

Organisation of This Book

This book is organised as follows. In the next chapter, we visit Hong Kong's early history starting from the Opium War that turned Hong

Kong into a British colony until the return of Hong Kong to Mainland China. Historically, Hong Kongers had a strong Chinese identity. There was a delicate balance achieved since Hong Kong's colonial period: British commercial interests made profits from Hong Kong, China utilised Hong Kong as a window to the world, and the Chinese in Hong Kong treated it as a safe harbour. Hong Kongers then focused on economics and they stayed apolitical.

Chapter 3 takes us through the 13 years from the Sino-British Joint Declaration to the handover in 1997. The Sino-British Joint Declaration in 1984 promised the full return of Hong Kong to the Chinese Mainland while China, and later the Basic Law, promised the people of Hong Kong to administer and preserve Hong Kong's government and legal system. The conditions agreed upon were: Hong Kong is an inalienable part of China, the Hong Kong Special Administrative Region will be directly under the authority of the Central People's Government of the PRC. The National People's Congress authorizes the Region to exercise a high degree of autonomy but the HK government will install laws to safeguard against subversion activities toward China's political regime. This chapter will hence describe the key contents in the document. Moreover, it documents important events. First, amidst the drafting of the Basic Law was the 1989 Tiananmen Square Crackdown which led to the formation of a core coalition suspicious of the CPC. Second, the British-Hong Kong Government introduced significant political changes. They led to the consolidation of a coalition opposing the CPC. They also totally liberalised the mass media creating what some would refer to as irresponsible publishing. Finally, they introduced a liberal welfare system which later led to social conflicts.

Chapter 4 describes the significant policies of the post-1997 Hong Kong Special Administrative Region (HKSAR) government and the impact of China's economic growth on Hong Kong. The chapter exposes the lack of consistency in the Hong Kong government's policies and Hong Kong's market-driven responses to China's economic growth. They inflicted stresses in Hong Kong's society, economically punishing many in the lower-income class. They deepened the social divide, which constituted serious roadblocks in building socio-political harmony in Hong Kong and in its integration with China.

Chapter 5 describes the rallies since 2000 and the latest in 2019. The severity of the rallies and protests created a blame narrative towards China and the establishment. They led to the 2019–2020 social unrest. Indeed, the organizers of the past rallies also organised the initial protests in 2019. The chapter then describes the trigger of the unrest. The chapter documents that the protests evolved into a violent anti-China, anti-CPC, and anti-government movement. The movement created an impression of police brutality, facilitated by the mass and social media, to sustain itself. The chapter raises questions on observable mass media bias which affects global opinions of the movement.

Chapter 6 questions the allegation that China has been repressing Hong Kong. Recorded documents reveal that China has been following the Basic Law. Although facts do not support the allegation, the allegation is successfully imprinted onto many Hong Kongers' minds. China has its share of missteps.

Chapter 7 drills into Hong Kong's accountability-light but blame-narrative-heavy opposition politics. The chapter reveals that the oft-cited "one-country, two systems" is only a vague concept. It is the Basic Law that defines the concept. The chapter explains that the Basic Law liberated Hong Kong from a colonial authoritarian system to let it have a democratic opposition politics for the first time. It also points out that Hong Kong does not have the eco-system to hold politicians accountable for their police-making bahaviour. This results in a dysfunctional brand of accountability-light opposition politics. The system let politicians pursue their interest instead of the public's interest. The Opposition and their allies promote a blame narrative against CPC, which inadvertently distracts attention from their inconsistent public policies. The right question to ask is why a narrative, basically a storyline, can maintain traction for so long. This leads us to Chapter 8 which discusses the linkage between social identity, education, and the level of intelligence in society. This could be the core reason for Hong Kong's failure on multiple fronts. Finally, the concluding chapter attempts to take stock and propose solutions for Hong Kong.

Chapter 2

The Beginning: History before 1982

This chapter provides a brief account of Hong Kong's history from the beginning of the colonial days to the 1970s. The historical facts usefully offer a glimpse of the perspectives of older Hong Kongers and Chinese at large. Firstly, the British government's colonisation of Hong Kong in 1842 was the beginning of China's century-long national humiliation. Secondly, partly related to Hong Kongers' discomfort with being colonial subjects, Hong Kong had multiple significant social unrests before and after WWII. However, Hong Kong bounced back strongly every time. Thirdly, a delicate compromise amongst Communist China, the British government, and Hong Kongers (who always kept a strong Chinese identity) maintained Hong Kong's stability. Within stability and the British legal institutions, generations of Hong Kongers worked extremely hard to deliver Hong Kong's economic growth.

China's Humiliation and Hong Kongers' Chinese Identity

China was the largest economy in the world for centuries until the earlier part of the 19th century. China's final imperial dynasty, the Qing (1644–1912), oversaw China's massive economic reversal and national humiliation. The dynasty entrenched a patronage-dependent Manchu elite (Brandt, Ma and Rawski, 2014),[4] held an aloof attitude towards Westerners who wanted to trade with China, and even towards missionaries. Many Chinese of the time thus also had a similar attitude towards "foreigners", preferring to hold on to their traditions rather than acknowledge the Western progress in technology and political systems.

Before the first Opium War (1839–1842), the dynasty isolated Western trade to Macau and a small sealed-off section of the riverbank in Guangzhou. Western merchants traded there with a small number of approved Chinese merchants. These state-sanctioned monopolists sold tea, silk, and other Chinese products to Western merchants for silver. Trade imbalance grew in favour of the Chinese. British merchants, such as the British East India Company, seeking a more advantageous medium of payment, began selling Indian opium to Chinese merchants.[5] This soon reversed the flow of silver (Brandt, Ma and Rawski, 2014). Realising opium was an addictive narcotic, China banned the opium trade and confiscated 1,400 tons of the drug stored in Canton by British merchants. Britain thus started a war with China which China lost. Under the Treaty of Nanjing, 1882, the Qing dynasty ceded Hong Kong Island to Britain and made large indemnity payments.[6]

---

[4] Loren Brandt, Debin Ma, and Thomas G. Rawski. 2014. "From Divergence to Convergence: Reevaluating the History behind China's Economic Boom", *Journal of Economic Literature* 2014, 52(1), 45–123.

[5] See, for example, https://www.britannica.com/topic/East-India-Company.

[6] This very unpleasant period in Chinese history would divert our attention from Hong Kong and we therefore delegate it to a footnote, taking advantage of materials from an unbiased account. The Encyclopedia Britannica (Kenneth Pletcher, ed.) reports:

"Foreign traders (primarily British) had been illegally exporting opium mainly from India to China since the 18th century, but that trade grew dramatically from about 1820. The resulting widespread addiction in China was causing serious social and economic disruption there. In Spring 1839 the Chinese government confiscated and destroyed more than 20,000 chests of opium — some 1,400 tons of the drug — that were warehoused at Canton (Guangzhou) by British merchants. The antagonism between the two sides increased in July when some drunken British sailors killed a Chinese villager. The British government, which did not wish its subjects to be tried in the Chinese legal system, refused to turn the accused men over to the Chinese courts. [...] Hostilities broke out later that year when British warships destroyed a Chinese blockade of the Pearl River (Zhu Jiang) estuary at Hong Kong. The British government decided in early 1840 to send an expeditionary force to China, which arrived at Hong Kong in June. The British fleet [...] attacked and occupied the city

That was the prelude to China's humiliating century of history: almost being partitioned and holding barely sub-colonial status, forced to accept the imposition of many unequal treaties, foreign concession

---

(Canton) in May 1841. Subsequent British campaigns [...] captured Nanjing (Nanking) in late August 1842, [...] resulting in the Treaty of Nanjing, signed on August 29 (1842). By its provisions, China was required to pay Britain a large indemnity, cede Hong Kong Island to the British, and increase the number of treaty ports where the British could trade and reside from one (Canton) to five (including Shanghai). [...] The British Supplementary Treaty of the Bogue (Humen), signed October 8, 1843, gave British citizens extraterritoriality [...] and most-favored-nation status [...]. Other Western countries quickly demanded and were given similar privileges."

A second Opium War broke out in 1856. Encyclopedia Britannic reports:

"The British, seeking to extend their trading rights in China, found an excuse to renew hostilities. In early October 1856 some Chinese officials boarded the British-registered ship [Chinese owned] *Arrow while it was docked in Canton, arrested several Chinese crew members (who were later released), and allegedly lowered the British flag. Later that month a British warship sailed up the Pearl River estuary and began bombarding Canton, and there were skirmishes between British and Chinese troops. Trading ceased as a stalemate ensued. In December Chinese in Canton burned foreign factories (trading warehouses) there, and tensions escalated. [...] The French decided to join the British military expedition, using as their excuse the murder of a French missionary in the interior of China in early 1856. [...] They* (British and French military) *captured Canton, deposed the city's governor, and in May 1858 allied troops reached Tianjin and forced the Chinese into negotiations. [...] The treaties of Tianjin, signed in June 1858, provided residence in Beijing for foreign envoys, the opening of several new ports to Western trade and residence, the right of foreign travel in the interior of China, and freedom of movement for Christian missionaries. In further negotiations in Shanghai later in the year, the importation of opium was legalized. The British withdrew from Tianjin in the summer of 1858, but they returned to the area in June 1859 en route to Beijing with French and British diplomats to ratify the treaties. The Chinese refused to let them pass by the Dagu forts at the mouth of the Hai River and proposed an alternate route to Beijing. The British-led forces decided against taking the other route and instead tried to push forward past Dagu. They were driven back with heavy casualties. The Chinese subsequently refused to ratify the treaties, and the allies resumed hostilities. In August 1860 a considerably larger force of warships and British and French troops destroyed the Dagu batteries, proceeded upriver to Tianjin, and, in October, captured Beijing and plundered and then burned the Yuanming Garden, the Emperor's summer palace. Later that month the Chinese signed the Beijing Convention, in which they agreed to observe the treaties of Tianjin and also ceded to the British the southern portion of the Kowloon Peninsula adjacent to Hong Kong."*

In 1898, Britain leased the territories north of Kowloon up to the Shenzhen river for 99 years, up to 1997.

areas, the colonisation of its territories including the northeastern provinces, Taiwan and many parts of western and south-western China.[7]

However, it was a time when the Western countries, and Japan later too, practised imperialism; China was not the only target. The desire to trade with China was natural as well. At the same time, China had its own problems. The Qing dynasty's mandarin court was divided, ignorant of reality, and generally not competent enough to deal with natural disasters (flood, drought, famine) and the shortage in government tax income.[8] A horrendous and costly civil war (the Taiping Revolution) showcased the Chinese people's dissatisfaction with the Qing court. Incidentally, the civil war drove many Chinese to move to Hong Kong. Qing-China genuinely needed modernisation: both for its economy and social-political system.

After the fall of the Qing dynasty in 1911, China was in a state of continuous internal conflicts. There was turmoil in establishing a Republic government: warlords were fighting against one another and the Kuomintang, and then the Kuomintang again with the Communist Party of China (CPC); then came the bloody Japanese invasion (1931–1945) and the continued fight between the Kuomintang and CPC (1946–1949) which ended in the establishment of the People's Republic of China (PRC) by the CPC in 1949. There was infamous corruption and hyperinflation during the Kuomintang regime, even when it was warring with Japan. Bolt, Timmer, and van Zanden (2014)[9]

---

[7] Chinese History was a required subject in Hong Kong's Secondary School Examinations for Certification of Education until 2011. This period in Chinese history had a strong emotional and identity effect on students in Hong Kong. Subsequently, Chinese History was no longer a required subject and became relegated to an unpopular elective. The exclusion of controversial subjects like the 1967 riots and the crackdown of the June 4th, 1989 Tiananmen protests from the history curriculum guidelines has been a thorny issue. (It should be noted though that exclusion from the guidelines, however, does not mean teachers do not have the rights to teach and discuss these topics.)

[8] Kangxi, the second Qing emperor (1661–1722) announced in 1712 that there would permanently be no increase in tax units, Qing taxes by household unit counts. This constrained the Qing dynasty's treasury options.

[9] Jutta Bolt, Marcel Timmer and Jan Luiten van Zanden. 2014. "GDP per capita since 1820", in Jan Luiten van Zanden, *et al.* eds. *How Was Life? Global Well-being since 1820*, OECD Publishing

report China's 1850 per capita GDP at $600 (1990 US dollars) and Japan's at $681. By 1950 China's per capita GDP was down 25.3% to US$448, while Japan's had risen 182% to $1,921.

After the establishment of the People' Republic of China, the CPC took part in the Korean War (June 1950–July 1953) and then made many disastrous economic policies and ill-fated political campaigns, including the Cultural Revolution. Miserably, all of these left China in 1978 a very poor country with a per capita GDP only 77% of India's GDP. However, by 1997, the year that Hong Kong re-unified with China, China's per capita GDP was US$781.64, 197% of India. China had begun recovery since the economic reforms in 1978, but the road was (and still is) long and hard.

During this difficult period, many Mainland Chinese went to Hong Kong as economic refugees, especially after 1949. Hong Kong's population increased from 2.057 million in 1951 to 4.697 million in 1978 and 6.3 million by 1997. More than 90% of Hong Kong residents were Chinese. Before the handover in 1997, Hong Kong was a safe harbour for them and yet their hearts were with China, always hoping that the motherland would eventually become successful. As in most other colonies, there was a very tiny fraction of Chinese who wanted to be seen as being of a "higher" class, mingling with the ruling British colonial master, and others from the Western countries. However, a great majority of Hong Kong Chinese shared the dream of Chinese around the world — a dignified and unified China with its population enjoying a stable and peaceful life.

British Hong Kong in Earlier Days: The 1956 and 1967 Riots

Britain's rule over Hong Kong was not a smooth ride. Britain ruled Hong Kong exactly as a colonial master would at the beginning, such as through racial zoning. Shortly after the New Territories was leased to Britain in 1898, the residents of Kam Tin (a village in Yuen Long which is a district in the New Territories) launched a "six-day war" of resistance in April 1899; it was suppressed by the British Army. On May 30th, 1925, after police under British command opened fire at a crowd of Chinese demonstrators in Shanghai, Canton and Hong Kong together launched a massive general strike to protest. More than 50,000 Chinese left Hong Kong, paralysing Hong Kong's economy, and trade fell by half. The British government injected a loan of 3 million pounds to save the economy and additionally sacked the two highest-ranked colonial officers for being out of touch.

After a brutal Japanese occupation, Britain reclaimed Hong Kong at the end of World War II. It was unclear how Britain and China settled on the future of Hong Kong; China was on the verge of another civil war (between the Kuomintang and the Communist Party). Many Chinese fled to Hong Kong before and after 1949, either through formal channels or as refugees. Many Shanghai companies moved to Hong Kong to escape communism. Thus, Hong Kong received a huge influx of labour, human capital, and financial resources from China, which significantly bolstered Hong Kong's growth. At the same time, China continued to export to Hong Kong its agricultural products. The freshwater from Dongjiang (the "East River," Canton Province) from 1960 onwards helped Hong Kong to alleviate its chronic water supply shortage which was essential for its development.

Hong Kong's Chinese residents at that time were divided in their political stances: pro-Nationalist and pro-Communist. An escalating provocation between the two camps on October 10th, 1956 ended in a riot which led to 59 deaths and approximately 500 injured. Riots erupted when a resettlement staff removed the Republic of China flag on October 10th which had been hung from a public housing project. The pro-Nationalists retaliated and riots erupted. The first few riots were fights between the pro-Nationalist and the pro-Communist members. Subsequently, the riots evolved to include anti-foreigner (non-Chinese) sentiments. Rioters in Nathan Road turned over and burnt a taxi carrying the Swiss Vice Council Fritz Ernst and his wife, who died in hospital two days afterwards. The riots were also a chance for rioters to vent their frustrations stemming from miserable living conditions. Premier Zhou En-lai of China issued a warning that China could neither ignore nor permit mistreatments of Hong Kong Chinese. The British-Hong Kong government called in extra manpower from the British Forces, including the famed armoured 7th Hussars troop. Peace was restored after estimated property damage of around US$1 million (about US$9.4 million today). A key outcome was that Hong Kong's Chinese residents saw themselves as all Chinese needing to make peace with one another, independent of their political stances.

The 1950s and early 1960s were a period of transformation in which Hong Kong expanded beyond being just an entrepôt. It developed vibrant labour-intensive manufacturing, supported by a large inflow of immigrants from China, many of whom crowded into make-shift huts of very poor quality and lived in squalid conditions. After a major fire in Shek Kip Mei which housed one of the hut clusters, the government launched subsidised multi-storey rental flats with very basic facilities.

In those days, Hong Kong was indeed a colony. Passports issued to Hong Kong Chinese named the holder a British subject. The British government maintained tight immigration control of Hong Kong residents.[10] British banks dominated financial markets and other British firms dominated property markets, trading, utilities, and transportation. Financial and political power was totally in the hand of the British government. Hong Kongers could not even dream of public health care and welfare. Churches provided a lot of social services, including education. The Royal Jockey Club provided a lot of charitable social services, including health care services.[11] Other charitable organisations, e.g., the Tung Wah Group of Hospitals, Po Leung Kuk (which protected abused women and children) also followed suit. Hong Kongers were self-reliant and hardworking. Many factory workers would work in the day and attend night school to learn English, the only official language. Ordinary Chinese could only envy the better treatment that non-colonial subjects enjoyed in Hong Kong.

An explicitly anti-government riot broke out in 1967, stemming from factory workers in Sun Po Kong who felt greatly ill-treated by their employers. That quickly escalated into anti-British protest rallies (and riots) organised by left-leaning labour unions. The objective can be interpreted as an attempt to turn Hong Kong away from British rule, just like slightly earlier riots turned Macau away from Portuguese rule. The rioters' acts of violence escalated, e.g., placing bombs in public areas and burning

---

[10] See Commonwealth Immigrants Act in 1962, 1968, Immigration Act 1972, Britain Nationality Act 1981, Hong Kong Act 1985 and British Nationality (Hong Kong Act) 1990.
[11] My primary education was only half-day, not full day.

a broadcaster to death.[12] The British-Hong Kong government again mobilised the British army and granted special powers to the police. It imposed a curfew and emergency regulations which included a mass control act to limit the number of people permissible in any public gathering (it was not relaxed until 1985). Anti-government newspapers were raided and some banned. China-owned departmental stores were searched. Some pro-CPC schools were shut down. Many leftist leaders were arrested, detained, and some later deported to the Mainland. Many well-to-do Hong Kongers migrated overseas. The riots lasted from May to October 1967. In total, 51 were killed and 15 by home-made bombs, 832 injured, 4,979 arrested, and 1,936 convicted, some were sent away to the Chinese Mainland. Property damage amounted to millions of dollars.

Chinese Identity, the Government's Reconciliation, and a Compromise

Allegedly, Premier Zhou En-Lai of the PRC asked the leftists in both the Mainland and Hong Kong to back off. CPC leaders recognised the importance of keeping Hong Kong as its window to the rest of the world and thus preferred to maintain Hong Kong's status quo as a British Crown colony. Hong Kong's existence was grounded on a political compromise — be China's window to the world, let Britain benefit from the colony, but make sure Hong Kong's people are taken care of, socio-economically speaking. Credit should go to the British-Hong Kong government for launching multiple welfare-improving adjustments, chief amongst which were the building of public housing, the cross-harbour tunnel, the subway system and the long series of comprehensive reforms which included anti-corruption reforms, establishing the famed Independent Commission Against Corruption (ICAC), developing District Councils, compulsory education, paid holidays, labour safety requirements, as well as homeownership schemes.

The British government continued to maintain a very high level of political control but made some modifications. The government

---

[12] A bomb placed in North Point's King's Road killed two innocent children; broadcaster Lam Bun and his cousin were set on fire on August 24th, 1967; Lam Bun died in a hospital on that day and his cousin a few days later.

maintained a *Political Department* (政治部) within the police force, which held anti-subversion operations as well as kept records of immigration, passports, and registration of persons.[13] While executive officers and permanent secretaries of ministries were appointed by Britain, there would be elected District Councils (which focused on community activities like sports and recreation). While there was strong supervision on sensitive subjects like Chinese history, including an indication of preferred wordings, (e.g., "Sino-British Trade War" was preferred to "Opium War,") it allowed Chinese history to be a compulsory subject in school. As far as I can tell, the Colonial government did not spend much effort on developing social identity but was always suspicious of movement to enhance the population's Chinese identity. However, school teachers were fond, proud even, of their Chinese identity. Some private schools handed out national flags (either the ROC or PRC national flag) to students.

The psyche of Hong Kong residents was interesting. They maintained their Chinese identity. Yet, many recognised the time was not right for reunification; China was undergoing internal political and economic turmoil. Hong Kong Chinese turned "apolitical" and focused on economics. Self-reliance was strong, they did not want to rely on social welfare, perceiving that as shameful. (Even now, some older people in Hong Kong feel ashamed to depend on Social Security payments and prefer to work menial jobs though they pay little.) The people worked incredibly hard and tried to make the best out of what was available. There was no voting, no democracy. The Crown Colony Affairs Office (and nominally the Queen) appointed and parachuted governors and ministers into Hong Kong and consulted perhaps only the British business leaders in Hong Kong. Hong Kong Chinese knew that if they worked for the government or a Western multinational firm, they would not be able to break through the ceiling defined by race and nationality. They also knew that the capital markets and real estate were dominated by British interests.

Yet, Hong Kongers often manifested their pride in being Chinese. They organised rallies to lobby for making Chinese an official language.

---

[13] The Department was rather secretive. The department and all its files were supposedly relocated before the handover. As an ordinary person, I did not have access to such privileged information.

They succeeded. Chinese became an official language in Hong Kong on March 23rd, 1974. They protested against Japan's territorial claiming of the "Diaoyutai" Islands (Senkaku Islands). These rallies were peaceful and civilised.

The British colonial government sustained the dominance of British commercial interests in Hong Kong. The mindset would be well illustrated by a conversation I had with a high-level executive in a British company in the early nineties (yes, that close to the handover year). I was an academic assigned to Hong Kong by a leading American business school to teach in an executive MBA program that the executive's company had sponsored. At the outset, the executive told me that senior managers were all Cambridge and Oxford graduates. Hong Kong university graduates supplied mid-level management to run the Hong Kong operations. Hong Kong thus existed in this type of compromise. Within this compromise, Hong Kong launched amazing growth. Its per capita GDP grew from US$723 in 1967 to US$6,134 in 1982 (current dollar) and it was widely lauded as one of Asia's economic miracles.

Summary

In summary, Hong Kong was colonised since 1842; but most of its residents were migrants, or refugees, from China. Hong Kong survived serious riots in 1956 and in 1967. The former was due to conflicts among Chinese with pro-KMT or pro-CPC stances. The latter was due to conflicts between labourers and employers that morphed into anti-government riots. They both contributed to a political and social equilibrium: Hong Kong existed as a colony catering to British and Western commercial interests, and China's only window to the rest of the world, and Hong Kong represented a safe harbour for the Hong Kong Chinese whose home country was in political and economic turmoil. Hong Kongers maintained a strong Chinese identity but focused on economics and stayed apolitical. The ruling British-Hong Kong government made welfare-enhancing reforms in Hong Kong. The equilibrium allowed Hong Kong's government, business, and people to cooperate to generate impressive economic growth.

Chapter 3

1982 to the 1997 Handover:
Distrust and Seeds for Trouble

Hong Kong grew substantially in the 1970s. It had a vibrant light manufacturing industry. It was also well positioned as the entrepot for the "China trade" as China started its economic reforms and growth. The symbiotic relationship between China, Hong Kong, and Britain deepened. Still, China's reforms were at the initial stage, and China would not be ready at all to absorb the international city that Hong Kong had become.

Britain started a secret discussion with China in 1979 about the future of Hong Kong, as the lease on Northern Kowloon and the New Territories signed in 1898 would expire in 1997. [14,15] For many Chinese, reunification, and maintaining the integrity of China's territories, was a non-compromisable primal objective — no Chinese leader would want to be blamed for failing in this respect. China's supreme leader, Mr. Deng Xiaoping, was adamant that the return of the whole of Hong Kong to the motherland was non-negotiable. Britain's Prime Minister Mrs. Margret Thatcher had confirmed that in her September 1982 visit to Beijing.

---

[14] The lease was signed at the Convention for the Extension of Hong Kong Territory on 9 June 1898 in Beijing.

[15] CNN, "The secret negotiations that sealed Hong Kong's future," (James Griffiths) June 22nd, 2017, https://edition.cnn.com/2017/06/18/asia/hong-kong-handover-china-uk-thatcher/index.html. This report was written based on de-classified documents.

The British Prime Minister Margaret Thatcher must have been surprised. Hong Kong's public was also taken aback, not just by the outcome, but also by the secrecy of the meeting. The HK dollar dropped like a rock and the government had to institute a peg with the US dollar (HK$7.8 per US dollar). Many in the upper-middle-class sought political hedge in the form of foreign passports. It is necessary to point out that Hong Kong had a tradition of outward migration of the rich and the capable due to their concerns about political uncertainties or their dislike of colonialism. Yet, Hong Kong continued to attract investors and human capital. Indeed, many who moved out and obtained foreign citizenship returned in the late 1980s and 1990s due to the Hong Kong economy's attractions, or because of their intrinsic feeling about being Chinese.

The British and the Chinese governments made the Sino-British Joint Declaration in 1984 to formalize the return of Hong Kong to China in 1997. Accordingly, this chapter focuses on critical developments from 1984 to 1997. The next section describes the gist of the Joint Declaration, including the essential elements stipulated to be included in the pending Basic Law. The section also explains that the point of contention amongst members of the Basic Law Drafting Committee was the approach to elect the Chief Executive and the Legislation Council members. Amidst the preparation of the Basic Law was the 1989 Tiananmen Square Crackdown. The crackdown raised the level of distrust of the CPC by Hong Kong representatives in the drafting committee. The third section describes vital elements of the Basic Law, the formal mini-constitution for the post-1997 Hong Kong. It is a thoughtful document which significantly elevates democracy in Hong Kong. Finally, the chapter presents the changes the last colonial government made in Hong Kong. These series of events, from the drafting of the Basic Law to the last governor's so-called "reforms", planted the seeds for Hong Kong's current political and economic troubles.

The Formation of the Basic Law: A Storm in the Middle

The Sino-British Joint Declaration regarding the future of Hong Kong was signed on December 19th, 1984. It is *"...a formal international agreement, legally binding in all its parts. An international agreement of this kind is the highest form of commitment between two sovereign states."*

The declaration states that the Hong Kong Special Administrative Region (HKSAR) shall be directly under the authority of the Central People's Government of the PRC from 1997 and the HKSAR shall enjoy a high degree of autonomy except for foreign and defence affairs. The HKSAR shall be allowed to have executive, legislative and independent judicial power following the British common law origin, including that of final adjudication. The government of the HKSAR from July 1st, 1997, will comprise local inhabitants. The Chief Executive is to be appointed by the Central People's Government based on the results of elections or consultations to be held locally. Principal officials have to be nominated by the Chief Executive of the HKSAR for appointment by the Central People's Government. Foreign nationals previously working in the public and police services in the government departments of Hong Kong can remain in employment. British and other foreign nationals can also be employed to serve as advisers or hold certain public posts in government departments of the HKSAR. These policies are to be included in the yet-to-be-drafted Basic Law of the Hong Kong Special Administrative Region; the Basic Law is to be vetted by PRC's National People's Congress. Furthermore, China's socialist system and policies are not to be practised in Hong Kong for 50 years from 1997. However, the Government of the United Kingdom is to be responsible for the administration of Hong Kong with the objective of maintaining and preserving its economic prosperity and social stability until 30th June, 1997 and the Government of the PRC is to give its utmost co-operation in this respect.

This declaration also regulates the right of abode and issuance of HKSAR passports. All Chinese nationals who were born or who have resided in Hong Kong for a continuous period of seven years or more are qualified to obtain permanent identity cards and an HKSAR passport. The same rights apply to their children even if they were born outside of HK. However, the entry of other Chinese into the HKSAR will continue to be regulated in accordance with the present practice.

China and Hong Kong leaders started the preparation, most importantly, the drafting of the Basic Law. The Drafting Committee (BLDC) was announced in Beijing in June 1985 as a working group under the National People's Congress (NPC) of the People's Republic of China. The BLDC was appointed by, and would report to, the NPC with a total of 59 members, 36 from the Chinese Mainland, and 23 from Hong Kong. The criteria for the Mainland members were familiarity with Hong Kong. Hong Kong members were seen as patriotic to China and had respectable professional knowledge of a particular sector. Some were legal and constitutional experts.

Among the 23 from Hong Kong were 12 tycoons, highly respected opinion leaders in the mass media sector, trade unionists, religious leaders, leaders of the original settlers in the New Territories, barristers, and the head of Hong Kong's teachers' union. From the outset, the debate was on the election of the Chief Executive and Legislative Council of the HKSAR. The business conservatives preferred selection through an electoral college and an executive-led system in which the executive would dominate the political system. The liberal professionals and grassroots organisations led by Seto Hwa and Martin Lee preferred direct elections for the Chief Executive, i.e., a fast pace formation of universal suffrage. (This tug of war is still ongoing.) In 1988, a "mainstream" model was proposed which was against an early introduction of direct elections for the Chief Executive and members in the Legislative Council but committed to universal suffrage ultimately.

As this debate went on, the crackdown of the 1989 June 4th Tiananmen Square student protest took place. A deep distrust of the Communist Party of China (CPC) emerged. Allegedly, 1.5 million Hong Kongers marched on the streets in Hong Kong to support the democracy movement on display in Tiananmen. (The actual number is likely less, but the majority of Hong Kongers clearly supported the democracy movement.) Eleven Hong Kong Basic Law drafters sent a joint letter to the central government calling for a faster pace of democracy in the city.[16] Afterwards, important members like Louis Cha (writer and owner of a newspaper), Szeto Wah (teacher), and Martin Lee (barrister) resigned from the BLDC.

---

[16] South China Morning Post, "June 4, 1989 events in China still have a profound effect on Hong Kong's political scene," (Gary Cheung) May 26th, 2013, https://www.scmp.com/news/hong-kong/article/1519713/june-4-1989-events-china-still-have-profound-effect-hong-kongs.

Still, the Third Session of the 7th National People's Congress held on April 4th, 1990 adopted the Basic Law, including the Method for the Selection of the Chief Executive and Formation of the Legislative Council. The Basic Law was promulgated by the President of the PRC as the Drafting Committee ceased to exist then.

Against this backdrop, it is clear that the Basic Law was formulated with some fraction of Hong Kong's people harbouring a suspicious attitude towards the Communist Party of China. Furthermore, in their minds, the integration was a golden opportunity to allow Hong Kong to have an election-based democracy (however undefined), something it never had during the colonial period and not supported even by the British-Hong Kong government's November 1984 "White Paper" on "Further Development of Representative Government in Hong Kong."[17] The next Governor, Chris Patten's actual actions (to be discussed in the section after the next) might have influenced them significantly. Possibly, to them, the June 4th, 1989 crackdown was frighteningly indicative of the CPC's strong desire to retain control at all costs; the image remained stuck in their minds. While scholars continue to debate whether universal suffrage generates democracy tax or dividends, ideology, not practical reality or pragmatism, drives passion.

The Key Elements of the Basic Law

The Basic Law is the Hong Kong Special Administration Region's mini-constitution; it is thoughtfully composed. It stipulates that Hong Kong is a part of China; it defines "one country, two systems" and that "Hong Kong people run Hong Kong." It promises Hong Kong universal suffrage, preserves Hong Kong's laws and autonomy, and develops a governance structure based on the separation of executive, legislative, and independent judicial power. The Basic Law also stipulates that members of its executive, as well as the Legislative and Judicial branches must swear to uphold the Basic Law and allegiance to the HKSAR of the PRC, and Hong Kong should disallow itself to be a base for destabilising China's government.

---

[17] The November 1984 White paper adopted the ideas of electoral college and functional constituents but concluded that there was no support for direct elections.

The Basic Law makes fundamental changes in Hong Kong's government structure. It effectively gives Hong Kong the democracy it never had during the British colonial time. During the colonial period, the British government appointed Hong Kong's governor with little Hong Kongers' involvement. In addition, during the colonial period, the governor appointed most members of the Legislative Council and chaired the Council. Thus, the British appointed governor had a concentration of power. The following will show that, according to the Basic Law, Hong Kongers are substantially involved in choosing the Chief Executive and in electing the Legislative Council members. Furthermore, the Basic Law weakens the Executive Branch's power and limits its freedom, relative to the colonial period. The next chapter explains that the Basic Law gives Hong Kong a form of democratic Opposition politics. Chapter 7 suggests that the Basic Law gives Hong Kong a theoretically workable democracy formula.

The following are key elements of the Basic Law:

- Hong Kong is a part of China: Article 1 stipulates that the Hong Kong Special Administrative Region is an inalienable part of the People's Republic of China.
- Hong Kong's autonomy: Article 2 stipulates that the National People's Congress authorises the Hong Kong Special Administrative Region to exercise a high degree of autonomy and enjoy executive, legislative and independent judicial power, including that of final adjudication, in accordance with the provisions of the Basic Law. (However, the power of interpretation of the Basic Law is vested in the Standing Committee of the National People's Congress in China.) Article 8 stipulates that there will be no change in Hong Kong's laws except for any that contravene the Basic Law, and subject to any amendment by the legislature of the Hong Kong Special Administrative Region. However, Article 12 stipulates that the HKSAR is directly under China's central government.[18] Article 18 stipulates that China's national laws shall not be applied in

---

[18] Article 22 stipulates that no department of the Central Government and any part of China can interfere with the Basic Law.

HK except for those listed in Annex III to the Basic Law, which encompass only defense and foreign affairs. However, the Standing Committee of the National People's Congress may add to or delete from the list after consulting its Basic Law Committee and the HKSAR government. This will be applicable if the Standing Committee of the NPC decides to declare a state of war, or, by reason of turmoil within the Hong Kong Special Administrative Region which endangers national unity or security and is beyond the control of the Region's government. (The establishment and enactment of the National Security Law in July 2020 is based on these clauses.)

- Government Structure: (i) executive power resides in the Executive Branch, (ii) legislative power resides in the Legislative Council,[19] and (iii) courts (from local to the court of final appeal) have independent judicial power including final adjudication.
- Election and appointment:

  - Article 45: The Chief Executive of the Hong Kong Special Administrative Region shall be selected by election or through consultations held locally and be appointed by the Central People's Government.[20] The method for selecting the Chief Executive shall be specified in the light of the actual

---

[19] This promise is reinforced by the following statement in the Basic Law: if any law enacted not in conformity with the provisions of the Basic Law regarding affairs within the responsibility of the central authorities or regarding the relationship between the Central and SAR, the Standing Committee of the National People's Congress may return the law but shall not amend it.

[20] Article 15 stipulates that the Central government appoint the CE and principal officials of the executive authorities in accordance with the provision in the Basic Law. Article 52 stipulates that the Chief Executive of the Hong Kong Special Administrative Region must resign under any of the following circumstances: (i) when he or she loses the ability to discharge his or her duties as a result of serious illness or other reasons; (ii) when, after the Legislative Council is dissolved because he or she twice refuses to sign a bill passed by it, the new Legislative Council again passes by a two-thirds majority of all the members the original bill in dispute, but he or she still refuses to sign it; and (iii) when, after the Legislative Council is dissolved because it refuses to pass a budget or any other important bill, the new Legislative Council still refuses to pass the original bill in dispute.

situation in the Hong Kong Special Administrative Region and in accordance with the principle of gradual and orderly progress. The ultimate aim is the selection of the Chief Executive by universal suffrage upon nomination by a broadly representative nominating committee in accordance with democratic procedures.

- Instruments 23 and 24, dated August 2014, state that Hong Kong was allowed to have universal suffrage in 2017 but the running candidates had to be nominated through a nomination committee, each with a simple majority of the committee's support.

• Article 68: The method for forming the Legislative Council shall be specified in the light of the actual situation in the Hong Kong Special Administrative Region and in accordance with the principle of gradual and orderly progress. The ultimate aim is the election of all the members of the Legislative Council by universal suffrage.

- Annex II specifies that (since 2007) there are 60 members in the Legislative Council; 30 members are selected by geographic constituencies via direct voting and another 30 selected via functional constituencies.

• The Hong Kong Judiciary is independent of both the Executive and the Legislative Branches of the HKSAR Government. The Chief Justice of the Court of Final Appeal is the head of the Judiciary. Under the Basic Law, judges are appointed by the Chief Executive of the HKSAR on the recommendation of the Judicial Officers Recommendation Commission. All judges and magistrates must have been qualified as legal practitioners either in Hong Kong or in another common law jurisdiction and have had substantial professional experience. The Basic Law stipulates that a judge may only be removed for inability to discharge his or her duties, or for misbehaviour, by the Chief Executive on the recommendation of a tribunal appointed by the Chief Justice of the Court of Final Appeal. This tribunal consists of not fewer than three local judges. In the case of dismissal of the Chief Justice, the tribunal (appointed by the Chief Executive instead of the Chief Justice) must consist of not fewer than five local judges. In addition, before a judge of the Court of Final Appeal or the Chief Judge of the High Court may be removed from office, the Basic Law stipulates that the endorsement of the Legislative Council is required.

- Furthermore, when assuming office, the Chief Executive, principal officials, members of the Executive Council and of the Legislative Council, judges of the courts at all levels and other members of the judiciary in the Hong Kong Special Administrative Region (HKSAR) must, in accordance with the law, swear to uphold the Basic Law of the HKSAR of the People's Republic of China and swear allegiance to the HKSAR of the PRC. (Hong Kong's Electoral Affairs Commission in 2016 disqualified six District Council election candidates for their refusal to sign the allegiant form or for explicitly advocating independence of Hong Kong on the grounds of violating the Basic Law. These decisions were deemed legitimate by Hong Kong's judiciary while candidates claimed violation of the Freedom of Speech.)

- Freedom of speech with conditionality: Article 27 stipulates that Hong Kong residents shall have freedom of speech, of the press and of publication; freedom of association, of assembly, of procession and of demonstration; and the right and freedom to form and join trade unions, and to strike. However, Article 23 stipulates that the Hong Kong Special Administrative Region shall enact laws on its own to prohibit any act of treason, secession, sedition, subversion against the Central People's Government, or theft of state secrets, to prohibit foreign political organisations or bodies from conducting political activities in the region, and to prohibit political organisations or bodies of the region from establishing ties with foreign political organisations or bodies. (An attempt to implement the article was the National Security Bill 2003 (Legislative Provisions) which led to a massive demonstration on July 1st, 2003. The bill was since shelved.)

- 2047: Article 5 makes a commitment that the socialist system and policies shall not be practised in the Hong Kong Special

Administrative Region, and the previous capitalist system and way of life shall remain unchanged for 50 years from 1997.

Chris Patten's "Political Reforms": The Formation of a Future Opposition Coalition

In 1984, the Hong Kong Government developed a "Green Paper" and then a "White Paper" on "Further Development of Representative Government in Hong Kong." The White Paper adopted the establishment of an electoral college and functional constituencies for electing unofficial members of the Legislative Council but concluded that there was little evidence of support in public comments for any move towards direct elections in 1985.[21]

The 1989 Tiananmen Square Protests changed the sentiments of Hong Kongers towards China. In 1992, British Prime Minister John Major removed Mr. Percy Cradock as Foreign Policy Adviser, and replaced former Hong Kong Governor David Wilson with the Conservative Party Chair Chris Patten, Patten thus became Hong Kong's last governor. (Chris Patten had just lost his seat in the British Parliament in the British 1992 elections.) At that point, the Legislative Council had 18 directly elected seats from geographical constituencies and 21 seats for functional constituencies to elect, and 17 governor-appointed seats. The Hong Kong Governor was the President of the Legislative Council and his chief secretary, attorney general, and financial secretary were ex-officio members with voting power. The Basic Law had already stipulated that post-1997, the Legislative Council would have 30 elected seats for geographical constituencies and 30 seats for functional constituencies.

With British Prime Minister John Major's support, Patten sought to make changes despite the established Basic Law and strong objections by previous Foreign Policy Adviser Percy Cradock, former Hong Kong Governors Murry MacLehose and David Wilson, and former Hong

---

[21] The Hong Kong Government (1984). White Paper: The Further Development of Representative Government in Hong Kong. Hong Kong: Government Printer.

Kong Chief Secretary David Akers-Jones. Chairing the Legislative Council, with help from his appointed council members and the ex-officio votes he had, Chris Patten passed a bill that: (i) broadened the definition of functional constituencies, (ii) allowed direct voting on many of these seats, and (iii) removed restrictions on the eligibility of candidates pursuing seats in the Legislative Council. (Note that under the Basic Law, the only viable change open to Chris Patten to make a lasting influence in the HK government's structure resided within the Legislative Council.) China deemed his moves as violating the Sino-British Joint Declaration in 1984. However, politicians supporting Patten won many seats in the 1995 election that Patten engineered.

Beijing created a Preliminary Working Committee on July 16th, 1993 which was dissolved in December 1995 and succeeded by the Preparatory Committee in 1996. The Preparatory Committee was responsible for implementation work related to the establishment of the HKSAR, including the establishment of the Selection Committee responsible for the selection of the first Chief Executive and the members of the Provisional Legislative Council. The Provisional Legislative Council replaced the Legislative Council elected in 1995. It repealed most of Patten's reforms.

This caused a scar in Hong Kong's politics that would be long-lasting. Beijing's nullification of Chris Patten's questionable changes in the selection of the Legislative Council likely strengthened the resolve of a group of politicians to be anti-CPC and to bring universal suffrage in choosing the Chief Executive and all the Legislative Council members. It is irrelevant to them that during colonial times, governors were directly appointed by Britain's Colonial Affairs and there was no election for the Legislative Council seats. Furthermore, the Tiananmen crackdown and China's reversal of Patten's changes (independent of whether they violated the Sino-British Joint Declaration) cemented their distrust of CPC. Henceforth, a fraction of Hong Kong politicians were bonded together by a fixation on universal suffrage and opposition to Beijing: a strong *opposition coalition* was born.

This faction of people did not represent Hong Kong. There was clear-cut evidence that in the past many in Hong Kong had a strong Chinese identity. They might or might not support the CPC, but they harboured no desire to topple CPC. They cheered for China's progress. That continued even after WWII and the 1967 riots. Hong Kongers lobbied and marched on the streets in the 1970s for Chinese to become an official language of Hong Kong and launched anti-Japanese protests over Chinese territorial issues. They welcomed the unification. However, a serious divisive undercurrent developed: the Opposition Coalition and their supporters vs at that time the majority of Hong Kongers. Families, whether at dining tables or over letters, discussed the reunification. There was some degree of apprehension but undeniably many factions of Hong Kongers accepted the outcome with positive expectations.

Two opposite stances loosely developed in Hong Kong after 1997: pragmatic gradualism blended with pro-economic growth and pro-China sentiments vs ideology-driven big-push for a loosely defined "democracy" based on anti-CPC and anti-establishment sentiments. People should have their freedom to act according to their convictions. The question is how differences in political stances are managed.

Unfortunately, the differences bred negative elements detrimental to Hong Kong's development of a coherent societal identity amiable to the "one country, two systems" concept. Furthermore, the government, run by politicians divided in their convictions but light in accountability towards people they were supposed to serve, had generated internally inconsistent policies that hurt the younger generation.

Other Changes that Created Forthcoming Challenges for Post-1997 Hong Kong

Before the handover, the British-Hong Kong government made a series of changes that created challenges for the post-1997 Hong Kong government. Here are some examples:

1. *Liberalised the control of the mass media and broadcasting*
   The British-Hong Kong government had always maintained strong control over the mass media. Since 1860, mass media publishers had to make a guarantee deposit which they could lose if successfully prosecuted

for libel. There were laws with simple procedures that applied for libel towards officials. In 1914, the government banned the mass media from publishing contents that created disturbance and subversion in Hong Kong or China. In the 1950s, the Governor could ban publications for posting hate statements towards the British royal family and the Hong Kong government. He could even order the suspension or cancellation of a publisher's registration. In 1967, in dealing with the leftist riots, besides imposing emergency laws and calling in the military, the government closed schools and newspapers that were anti-government. The rules set in 1936 regarding radio broadcasting and in 1964 regarding broadcasting gave the Hong Kong government widespread power to monitor and restrict commentaries and editorials, including the power to cancel publication or broadcasting rights.

The Hong Kong Legislative Council in 1987 abolished fake news regulations[22] on the grounds that everyone is entitled to personal opinions and is innocent until proven guilty. (This argument is faulty. Fake news and libels are civil cases that do not involve the concept of innocent until proven guilty, unlike in criminal cases. Also, it would be up to the prosecutor to show evidence that incorrect news was released or that the statements that were made public thereafter lowered the standing of the plaintiff amongst right-minded people.) Similarly, regulations and monitoring of publications and broadcasting were liberalised on the grounds that many of the past regulations and laws were meant to deal with subversive forces and Hong Kong had not had to enforce the regulations since 1967. (This argument is illogical; the law did not need to be invoked precisely because it was effective in deterring offenses.) The Legislative Council discussion went on to claim that times had changed, and that Hong Kongers wanted more freedom of speech and press. (The reality is

---

[22] South China Morning Post, "Has fake news, spread by social media, led to the riots we see today? If so, has free speech failed?" (Andrew Sheng) October 26th, 2019, https:// www.scmp.com/comment/opinion/article/3034426/has-fake-news-spread-social-media-led-riots-we-see-today-if-so-has. See also https://www.legco.gov.hk/yr01-02/chinese/bc/ bc59/papers/bc590614cb2-2283-1c.pdf.

that the proliferation of the internet facilitated the exponential growth of fake news.)

Since the 1990s, some of Hong Kong's mass media have embraced tabloid journalism. Beginning with uncovering some scandals linked to politicians and celebrities, they continued by taking a lurid approach towards China and the Hong Kong government. In fact, in the 1950s and 1960s, when government control was tight, newspapers took on a political stance: pro-CPC, pro-Kuomintang, pro-British-HK government, etc. However, they were reserved and measured under the British controlling laws, especially after 1967. Since the 1990s, the mass media in Hong Kong appears to have become much less so; but the speculation needs empirical investigation. In the current era, exaggerated news and fake news often appear in social media. Globally, the mass media adopts emotion-rousing and "screaming" headlines and often prints even blatantly distorted reports. I suspect that these create noise and hinder the seeking of facts. In Hong Kong, mass and social media amplify emotions and have affected the work both in the Executive and Legislative Branches after 1997. We need careful empirical research, however, to establish causality.

2. *Started welfare programmes*

For years, Hong Kong had limited public assistance despite high-income inequality, e.g., the Gini from 1981 to 1986 was 0.45. The world praised Hong Kong for practising a non-interventionist small government economic philosophy. However, in 1993, the very limited public assistance scheme was renamed the *Comprehensive Social Security Assistance* (CSSA) scheme with a considerable increase in benefits. (The payment for those who passed the low household income and asset holding test was set at HK$2,000/month per head. There would also be various supplements related to long-term care, single parenthood, age, and disability.) Also, the residency requirement was only 1 year. Within 1993, there was an increase in CSSA cases by 15% and expenditure by 54.9%. CSSA cases rose from 79,700 cases at the beginning of 1993 to 195,645 in 1997 (an increase of 145%). These changes to the CSSA might well have triggered an influx of immigrants from the Mainland, raised government expenditures, and created social tensions. (The payment appeared to be very generous to the comparatively poorer Chinese. Even in 1997, China's GDP per capita was RMB521 per month, which is about 25% of HK$2,000.) The program's impact on Hong Kong's society was considerable as we shall see in the next chapter.

Summary

In the 1980s, many Hong Konger welcomed the scheduled return of Hong Kong to China in 1997 and the 1984 Sino-British Joint Declaration. At the same time, some were apprehensive. Many among the elites and wealthy moved abroad and returned after they had obtained foreign passports ("political hedge"). The drafting of Hong Kong's Basic Law was interrupted by the June 4th, 1989 political storm in China. Many observers correspondingly developed a deep distrust of how the Communist Party of China might handle dissidents. However, the Basic Law is a thoughtful document which gives the post-1997 Hong Kong a level of democracy it never had during the British colonial era. Starting in the mid-1980s, the British contemplated political reforms in Hong Kong which were intensified in the 1990s. The last Governor Chris Patten's 1994 attempt to change the formation and memberships of the Legislative Council was nullified by China. However, this cemented for Hong Kong the development of an opposition coalition against CPC and pro-China policies. The liberalisation of mass media control unleashed a platform for vociferous opposition. The more generous welfare programmes attracted many lower-income Chinese migrants from the Mainland. This subtly changed the mindsets of Chinese immigrants and Hong Kongers' perceptions of them. All these became seeds for the social and political discordances that have been affecting Hong Kong's journey since 1997.

Chapter 4

Post-1997: An Era of Inconsistent Policies

Hong Kong's return to China was an uncharted human journey. In 1997, both Chinese leaders and Hong Kong politicians were inexperienced. Indeed, there was no historical precedent on integrating a very Westernised capitalist metropolitan into a huge communist country striving to modernise. The guideline of "preserving Hong Kong's system for 50 years" is too general to be practical. What exactly is "Hong Kong's system?" The oft-cited "one country, two systems" is not a road map, just a concept — "one country" means Hong Kong is an inalienable part of China, "two systems" means China has a socialist system and Hong Kong has a capitalist system.

The vague concept needs a workable definition. The Basic Law does the job. Article 5 is a commitment that China's socialist system and policies shall not be practised in the Hong Kong Special Administrative Region, and Hong Kong's previous capitalist system and way of life shall remain unchanged for 50 years. The Basic Law defines the government structure: (i) executive power resides in the Executive Branch, (ii) legislative power resides in the Legislative Council,[23] and (iii) courts (from local to the court of final appeal) have independent judicial power including final adjudication. ***The preservation of "one country,***

---

[23] We reiterate here, as stated in footnote 19, that this promise is reinforced by the following statement in the Basic Law: if any law enacted is not in conformity with the provisions of the Basic Law regarding affairs within the responsibility of the Central authorities or regarding the relationship between the Central and SAR, the Standing Committee of the National People's Congress may return the law [for reconsideration] but shall not amend it.

two systems" is to follow the Basic Law, and that is the one and only definition of preserving "one country, two systems."

By design, the Basic Law has changed Hong Kong's government system. It liberated Hong Kong from a colonial system that ruled Hong Kong up to the July 1st 1997 handover. During the Colonial period, governors were appointed by the British Colonial Foreign Affairs Office, with the exception of the last governor Chris Patten, who was directly appointed by the British Prime Minister John Major. The governor chaired both the Executive Branch and the Legislative Council. He also appointed many "official" members in the Legislative Council and had multiple ex-officio votes. (This information was included even in primary school textbooks in Hong Kong in the 1960s.) Essentially, the British-appointed governor controlled both the Executive Branch and the Legislative Councils and was directly accountable only to the British government; Hong Kongers were at best consulted but not necessarily listened to. For example, the forced replacement of Sir David Wilson by Chris Patten was unwelcomed.[24]

The Basic Law has created a political system that empowers the Legislative Council in the sense that it can get rid of the Chief Executive. Article 52 stipulates that the Chief Executive of the Hong Kong Special Administrative Region must resign under any of the following circumstances: (i) when he or she loses the ability to discharge his or her duties as a result of serious illness or other reasons; (ii) when, after the Legislative Council is dissolved because he or she twice refuses to sign a bill passed by it, the new Legislative Council again passes by a two-thirds majority of all the members the original bill in dispute, but he or she still refuses to sign it; and (iii) when, after the Legislative Council is dissolved because it refuses to pass a budget or any other important bill, the new Legislative Council still refuses to pass the original bill in dispute. The Basic Law has introduced a form of democratic "opposition politics" in Hong Kong that it has hitherto never experienced.

---

[24] South China Morning Post, "David Wilson was forced out as governor of Hong Kong by British prime minister John Major despite objections from Executive Council, new declassified files reveal." January 2nd, 2019, https://www.scmp.com/news/hong-kong/article/2180311/david-wilson-was-forced-out-governor-hong-kong-british-prime-minister.

In this context, Hong Kong has to engineer a path towards fuller integration before the pre-set 2047, the year in which Beijing has the option to fully take over, as agreed in the 1984 Sino-British Joint Declaration. How may the government engage a traditionally apolitical population to meaningful conversations in order to chart Hong Kong's path forward? Well-intended and informed discussions within the government, amongst the educated, the business leaders, and the public, as well as cross-group consultations, would be tremendously useful. The leaders of the various interest groups in Hong Kong need to engage in effective communication with the masses, not only to allow content exchanges but also emotional bonding imperative for identity building.

The problem is that Hong Kong's leaders, whether they are in the Executive Branch or the Legislative Council, are inexperienced in opposition politics. The developments before 1997 documented in the previous chapter have made Hong Kong's journey particularly treacherous. As the previous chapter documented, a hardened opposition group held a rebellious attitude towards China's CPC and the establishment. It could and did use the new government structure to pursue their private political goals. The change in Hong Kongers' perception of immigrants from the Mainland became the basis of destructive identity politics unfavourable to China. The liberalised mass media was able to amplify cynicism and identity politics. Social media, which would become prevalent later, was able to be the conduit for the formation of evidence-light destructive blame narratives. In other words, the discordance between the hardened opposition and the establishment, and the hitherto unseen suspicion by Hong Kongers of fellow Chinese from the Mainland, became detrimental to Hong Kong's development of a coherent society amiable to the "one country, two systems" concept.

The issue is not about the presence of opposition politics. It is about how disagreements and debates are managed. Accountability matters. Politics with accountability allows opposition to constructively constrain poor policymaking. However, the outcome would be different if ability to discipline politicians' inappropriate behaviours is lacking. Politicians on both sides would become self-serving rather than public-serving.

Would the opposition politics in Hong Kong lead to a constructive or destructive evolution for Hong Kong? This is what the whole world wants to know. Time will tell. Unfortunately, since 1997, the discordance among different camps has contributed to a series of amazingly incoherent and inconsistent post-1997 government policies that only add stress to Hong Kong's society, especially the lower-income class.

A Glorious Record but Inconsistent Policies

Before we discuss these, I should point out some of Hong Kong's significant achievements. Firstly, from 1997 to 2018, despite the Asian Financial Crisis in 1997 and an epidemic (SARS) in 2003, Hong Kong's per capita GDP grew from 2.8–2.9% in constant dollar or in purchasing power adjusted terms. While this was almost identical to that of Taiwan, it was noteworthy that Hong Kong's per capita GDP was almost double that of Taiwan.[25] So, Hong Kong's growth was much more substantial. Secondly, Hong Kong saw a steady increase in life expectancy, from 80.13 years in 1997 to 84.23 years in 2016, which is the highest in the world. CNN reported on March 2nd, 2018 that Hong Kong's life expectancy was globally the highest and gave credit to Hong Kong's green environment, universal health care for hospital treatment, and familial values.[26] Indeed, Hong Kong's accomplishments in infrastructure development, public transportation, and universal health care (for hospital treatments) seemed almost magical, especially to those who lived through the sixties and seventies when raw sewage was dumped into Hong Kong harbour and heavy traffic jams immobilised people and disrupted lives.

Unfortunately, Hong Kong's public policies since 1997 were internally inconsistent which exerted tremendous pressures on

---

[25] For example, according to CEIC data, Taiwan's and Hong Kong's per capita GDP in constant US dollars in 2018 were 25,026 and 48,684, respectively. HK's number is 1.95 of Taiwan's. The comparison is amazing because it is well known that higher income countries often grow at a slower rate.

[26] See https://www.cnn.com/2018/03/02/health/hong-kong-world-longest-life-expectancy-longevity-intl/index.html.

Hong Kong as a society. Hong Kong offered a generous welfare hand-out programme accessible to immigrants, thus attracting economic immigrants whom a significant proportion of Hong Kongers did not welcome. The programme predictably raised the demand for medical and social services, as well as affordable housing. Yet, Hong Kong did not increase the supply of doctors and public housing. On the contrary, the elimination of residential rent control further tilted housing supply towards the high-end. The free market policy tolerated property tycoons' hoarding of land and this jacked up housing costs further. Everyone except the rich was aggrieved, and it further aggravated the negative attitude towards immigrants from the Mainland.

In a bid to adjust to China's phenomenal growth since its economic reform, Hong Kong's manufacturing sector and its jobs moved to the Mainland given the lower wages and land costs there. At the same time, Hong Kong's open financial and human capital market policy allowed Hong Kong to serve as a key financial hub in Asia and particularly for the fast growing China. The financial sector's success further raised Hong Kong's land cost and salaries of its employees. However, the open-door policy intensified job competition at the high end for young university graduates. The escalating business real estate rental exerted downward pressure on profits for small businesses and salaries of the unskilled.

China could well be made a scapegoat for these economic stresses. However, it is important to remember that behind the stresses was the inconsistent policies. Hong Kong attracted economic immigrants but stopped short at providing them affordable housing. Hong Kong adopted a free-market policy that favoured capitalists and made Hong Kong is to China what Manhattan is to the US, but failed in offering matching policies to integrate Hong Kong with China. Crucially, the government lacked a coherent long-term plan for Hong Kong, especially its future generation.

In the following section, we shall examine all of these shockingly inconsistent policies that hollowed out economic opportunities in the middle, dimmed the younger generations' outlook on life, and resulted in rising socio-political discordance in Hong Kong.

Immigrants from China and Population Growth

By any standards, Hong Kong is a small city with a high population density. Since 1997, there has been huge inward immigration to Hong Kong from the Mainland. *The Economist* suggested that *"since Hong Kong returned to Chinese sovereignty in 1997, around 1m Mainland Chinese have immigrated to Hong Kong [...] accounting for 90% of the city's population growth in recent years."*[27] The total number of immigrants, of course, is even greater because of immigrants from South Asia. Hong Kong's official population statistics are as follows: 6.3 million in 1997, 7.372 million in 2018, and 7.458 million in 2019.

Such a high influx of immigrants could stress any society. Depending on how one considers the statistics, the number may not seem too extraordinary. For example, when tallied by the number of all migrants per 1,000, Hong Kong was way below Macau, Singapore, Canada, and the US, amongst others. However, when tallied by the number of newly arrived immigrants per 1,000 from 1997 to 2018, Hong Kong had 138.68/1000, which was amongst the highest in the world, based on World Bank data published in 2019.

As previously mentioned, the large influx of mainland immigrants was driven by policies set up before the 1997 handover. The 1984 Sino-British Joint Declaration stated that from 1997 onwards, the children of Hong Kong permanent residents of Chinese nationality, who were born outside of the territory, would have the right of abode in Hong Kong. Many Hong Kong males, particularly from the class of unskilled labour, went back to China to get married. The General Household Survey of 1991 estimated that more than 95,000 Hong Kong residents were married in Mainland China with their spouses still there. Adding their children and accumulation over time, this number could easily become hundreds of thousands. The *Comprehensive Social Security Assistance* programme, established in 1993, had only a one-year residency requirement for benefits. The generous handout of

---

[27] The Economist, "An influx of mainland Chinese is riling Hong Kong," October 20th, 2018, https://www.economist.com/china/2018/10/20/an-influx-of-mainland-chinese-is-riling-hong-kong.

HK$2,000 per month was four times China's per capita income; it provided the financial incentive for families to reunite in Hong Kong.

Chief Executive Tung Chee-Hwa was concerned about the inward migration rate. He raised the residence requirement to seven years in 2004, hoping to slow down the inflow. The Opposition objected. Later, in December 2013, Hong Kong's Court of Final Appeal ruled CE Tung's amendment to be unconstitutional. The government reverted to the one-year residence requirement for CSSA qualification.

Another immigration-related concern is that Hong Kong attracted "birth tourism" from the Mainland. Hong Kong's free universal hospital care services included the delivery of babies. Also, Hong Kong did not have a one-child policy. In the Mainland, the one-child policy which was in force at the time meant that every household could only have one child. Delivering a baby in Hong Kong allowed people to bypass official birth registration in China. Furthermore, a baby born in Hong Kong to two Mainland parents, neither of whom was a Hong Kong resident, was entitled to the right of abode. The Hong Kong Executive Branch tried to change these practices but the Opposition objected. In a 2001 case, the *Court of Final Appeal* ruled that such babies indeed had the right of abode in Hong Kong.[28] Mainland pregnant women were thus attracted to give birth to their babies in Hong Kong. Consequently, a very large fraction of the babies born in Hong Kong were to Mainland couples, which caused high social tension.[29] To limit Mainland mothers travelling over to Hong Kong to give birth, starting February 1st, 2007, pregnant women from the Mainland had to pay $5,000 for their hospital care even before they were allowed to enter Hong Kong. Against the wish of some Opposition legislators, HK's Chief Executive imposed effective administrative measures to substantially reduce such births in HK, e.g., the Hospital Authority imposed quotas on Mainland women giving birth in public hospitals, raised fees for them, raided unlicensed hostels that

---

[28] Director of Immigration v. Chong Fung Yuen, 2001. The number of babies born to mainland mothers soared to 20,000 in the first 10 months of 2006 from less than 9,000 in 2002.

[29] BBC, "Hong Kong to limit mainland China maternity services," April 25th, 2012, https://www.bbc.com/news/world-asia-china-17838280.

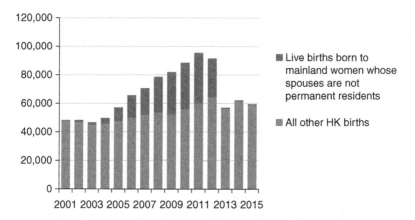

Figure 1. Hong Kong births.

Source: HKSAR Census and Statistics Department.

provided accommodation to the expectant mothers from the Mainland. Starting in 2012, Mainland women would be prevented from giving birth in Hong Kong unless they have a Hong Kong husband. Figure 1 shows the historical pattern of live births born to Mainland women whose spouses are not Hong Kong citizens or permanent residents. Even though eventually stopped, the influx was immense.

There were other immigrants too. A foreign worker with no criminal record working for more than seven years in Hong Kong could obtain the right of abode. Somehow, this was not extended to foreign domestic helpers. The Opposition promoted extending the right to them. On September 30th, 2011, the Hong Kong Court of First Instance issued a landmark decision that a law prohibiting foreign domestic helpers from acquiring permanent residency in Hong Kong was unconstitutional.[30]

The tug of war between the Executive Branch, which tried to contain the influx of immigrants and non-Hong Kong residents consuming

---

[30] A lawyer stated that "it is believed that some 117,000 would, based on this ruling, automatically acquire the right to apply for permanent residency, having met the requirement of living in Hong Kong for a continuous period of at least seven years." (Latham & Watkins, The Working World, Issue 14, March 2012), https://www.lw.com/thoughtleadership/landmark-right-of-abode-ruling-for-foreign-domestic-helpers-in-hong-kong.

Hong Kong's free hospital services, and the Opposition, which was "pro-immigration" and "human rights", was energy draining.

Embracing human values of care is applaudable. However, the government and society have to make sufficient preparations and accommodate changes. Hong Kong failed to do so. The Opposition took an active pro-immigration policy stance at the beginning. However, they later objected to the Executive Branch's policy to provide affordable housing to lower-income people. Some even openly embraced anti-immigrant policies. Meanwhile, the Executive Branch practiced free-market principles which led to housing development biased against the poor and the young. Hong Kong's high per capita GDP growth masked these miseries inflicted on the non-rich by fighting politicians' inconsistent policies. I shall elaborate further.

The Government CSSA, Economic Immigrants and Social Sentiment

Before turning to that, we need to discuss the impact of the immigration policy on social sentiment. In the past, Hong Kong had also taken in refugees or economic immigrants from the Chinese mainland; but all entrants then had to make a living on their own. Hence, they contributed to Hong Kong's economic growth, and Hong Kong residents accommodated them. After the installation of the *Comprehensive Social Security Assistance* (CSSA) scheme (as described in the previous chapter), a significant portion of the migrants entered Hong Kong because of the welfare payments and free hospital care. The CSSA payment per qualified person was HK$2,000/month, and there were add ons like transportation support. The money, being four times China's per capita GDP in 1997, was a huge economic attraction to lower income Chinese, especially to those in China's rural areas.

CSSA cases (established in 1993) increased from 195,645 in 1997 to 288,648 in 2003, a 48% increase. The budget rose from HK$9.4 billion in 1998 to HK$16 billion in 2002, a 70% increase. From 1997–8 to 2003–4, expenditure on social welfare significantly increased from 1.6%

to 2.7% of Hong Kong's GDP. Out of the social welfare expenditure, CSSA accounted for 31.6% in 1992–3 and rose to 72.8% in 2001–2. The increase was mostly driven by immigrants and an aging population. While these numbers were unlikely to stress Hong Kong's government budget, they received attention. Newspaper headlines speculated that the CSSA drove up Hong Kong's welfare payment to the extent of more than 1% of GDP.[31]

Traditionally, Hong Kong was a society that did not depend on welfare payments. The older generation of Hong Kongers especially saw collecting welfare payments as something shameful. Over time, Hong Kongers developed a negative impression of economic immigrants from the Mainland. The mass media often mocked the Mainlanders' behaviour, e.g., their hygiene habits and their accent. Some Hong Kongers employed explicitly insulting terms, e.g., locusts, to describe them. The significant and non-gradual rise in CSSA cases was also burdensome to social workers, affecting their performance and their attitude towards Mainland Chinese.

Even today, children of "new immigrants" are often bullying targets in schools. This may be rather universal and school bullies everywhere pick on immigrants. However, instead of working to mitigate the problem, the Opposition disregarded its prior pro-immigration stance, and turned to aggravate the problem. Some explicitly promoted nativism to deepen the anti-Mainland Chinese sentiment. For example, some in the pro-democracy camp established a "Hong Kong First" party in 2013 claiming to promote localism to safeguard Hong Kong's high degree of autonomy and lifestyle. The Party sponsored "Hong Kong First ads" that HK's Equal Opportunity Commission condemned as discriminatory.

Due to politics, Hong Kong did not prepare well for the influx of immigrants, which easily ranged from 15% to 20% of its population. Many of the Mainland immigrants in those days were of lower economic

---

[31] Hung Wong (2012) "Changes in Social Policy in Hong Kong since 1997: Old Wine in New Bottles?" Wai Man Lam, Percy Luen-tim Lui and Wilson Wong (eds) *Contemporary Hong Kong Government and Politics,* Hong Kong University Press, p. 277.

means, joining families of similar status. The same consideration may apply to immigrants who work as domestic helpers. Practising care has to come with matching government policies. It is more than obvious that these would increase welfare spending and the need for public medical services and housing.

Medical Services

The Public Medical Services sector has been overloaded for a long time. The South China Morning Post reported on February 26th, 2019 that, *"... demand for medical services in the city has exploded. From 2007 to 2017, the population grew by about 7% to 7.4 million, with a much higher proportion of people aged 65 or above, and life expectancy has risen to 82 years for men and 88 years for women."*[32] Scheob (2016) described the shortage of health professionals:

> *"Medical services are already sometimes understaffed but will be short of medical professionals in the near future. [...] the Hong Kong government has allowed the [city's] two medical schools to increase the number of medical school graduates from 250 last year to 420 by 2018. Additional measures are to increase the retirement age for medical doctors [...] and to allow overseas doctors to take jobs at public hospitals on a special temporary license, renewed annually by the Medical Council. However, access to practice for foreign-trained medical doctors is limited, as they have to apply for registration by passing a three-part exam (professional knowledge, English, and clinical examination) and participate in a 12-month internship before they can become registered. A reform to address the composition of the Medical Council in order to improve its efficiency in handling complaints and thereby to enhance transparency was blocked by medical professionals and the Legislative Council (LegCo). This failed attempt to reform the Medical Council demonstrates the tension between*

---

[32] South China Morning Post, "Hong Kong's health care system is teetering on the brink. What's wrong with it, what can be done to fix it and will the budget provide some answers?" February 26th, 2019, https://www.scmp.com/news/hong-kong/health-environment/article/2187630/hong-kongs-health-care-system-teetering-brink.

rationally solving the staff shortage crisis by giving access to potential entrants and keeping the exclusive status of the medical profession."[33]

There are other areas of shortage, e.g., hospital staff and administrators. Heavy paperwork does not help either, as the medical service sector has pointed out. Utilisation of medical coupons, which can divert unnecessary emergency room visits to private clinical facilities, was only introduced in 2009 for residents older than 70 (the age was lowered to 65 in 2017). The *Voluntary Health Insurance Scheme* offered since April 2019, expands private coverage to the age of 100 regardless of the change in health condition and covers unknown pre-conditions and with no limit on lifetime benefit. These are steps in the right direction, albeit latecoming. The question remains: how will Hong Kong meet the demand for medical services if there is no fundamental increase in supply? That said, many observers would point out that Hong Kong's public health care and coverage is already the envy of many countries (and far better than during the colonial era).

As mentioned, we have to question the government's preparedness and agility in responding to predictable needs. The influx of immigrants and ageing has been totally predictable. By way of illustration, the two medical schools in Hong Kong were both established in the colonial era (HKU's medical college in 1887 and CUHK in 1981. HKU is now planning a new medical school in Shenzhen). By contrast, Singapore has a smaller population but more medical schools that graduate more doctors. In 2018, the populations of Singapore and Hong Kong were, respectively, 5.8 million and 7.5 million. Singapore has 3 medical schools. In 2018, it graduated 428 doctors and accepted 500 new students. Hong Kong's number was 420 doctors in 2018. Why has Hong Kong not trained more doctors?

There could of course be other solutions. To alleviate possible doctor shortage, Singapore allows medical school graduates from 103 foreign countries to practise in Singapore, the list includes the two

---

[33] Veronika Schoeb (2016) "Healthcare Service in Hong Kong and its Challenges: The Role of Health Professionals within a Social Model of Health," *China Perspectives* 2016(4).

medical schools in Hong Kong. On the contrary, Hong Kong erects high entry barriers for foreign-trained doctors to serve in Hong Kong, as described by Scheob (2016), despite its very low doctor to population ratio (1 to 519) and the ever-increasing demand due to immigration and an ageing population. Let me illustrate further by citing Dr. Ronald Ng, a practising *haematologist* in Singapore who practised in Hong Kong and London before:

> *"If a top specialist, say in heart surgery, wants to practise in Hong Kong, he or she is required to sit an exam which would include questions on obstetrics, paediatrics, etc. — areas which he or she has studied as an undergraduate but has since forgotten as he or she has to specialise in heart surgery. Is he or she going to spend time reviewing and memorising those subjects just to pass the exam in order to practise heart surgery? It is, therefore, a strong barrier for specialists to come to Hong Kong. […] The Hong Kong Medical Council's argument of maintaining standards is just another fanciful protectionist barrier. Singapore has solved, to a very large extent, its shortage of medical practitioners in the public sector by adopting these common-sense practices. Perhaps Hong Kong should learn from that. As someone who used to work and teach in Hong Kong and London as a medical professional and now active in a similar role in Singapore, I know they will work equally well in Hong Kong. The industry leaders should stop hiding their narrow self-interest behind flimsy protectionist barriers that can only hurt the public good."*[34]

These entry barriers to practise medicine in Hong Kong are of course promoted by the medical establishment. The pro-government Democratic Alliance for the Betterment and Progress of Hong Kong (DAB) had proposed removing the licensing exams for foreign-trained doctors, but the idea met with strong opposition from members of the medical community.[35] The medical functional constituent

---

[34] China Daily, "Barriers need to be eased for overseas medical graduates," (Ronald Ng) April 12th, 2019, https://www.chinadailyhk.com/articles/185/235/113/1555000891234.html.
[35] South China Morning Post, "Hong Kong doctors support exempting foreign-trained professionals from internship requirement in bid to solve crippling doctor shortage," April

representative, MD Pierre Chan, a younger generation doctor in the Opposition camp elected to the Legislative Council in 2016, took an oppositional stance.[36] His fellow pro-democracy camp colleagues supported his stance. The Medical Council, the independent body that licenses doctors, voted on May 8th, 2019 not to make changes.

One has to wonder why the government machinery cannot make efficient and effective adjustments in a more expedient and timely manner. One also has to wonder why various medical boards and associations take rigid positions in defending their monopolist positions and why the Opposition sides with them. The Opposition promoted immigration in the past and claimed to work for the non-established. One has to ask why it would align with the medical establishment that has vested market power (and doctors have high income), at the expense of people they claim to work for? (It possibly values saying no to the Executive Branch more than serving the people.) We also have to think about how the average Hong Konger would feel about the surge in demand for public medical service. Whom would he or she blame for this situation: the legislators or the fellow Chinese they called "locusts" from the Mainland?

Housing Shortage and Cost

An influx of about 1 million immigrants to any city, many of whom are not high-income earners, would undoubtedly raise the demand for affordable housing. The surge in Hong Kong's housing cost is globally known. There is a lot of negative publicity regarding Hong Kong's housing affordability. For example, the *15th Annual Demographic International Housing Affordability Survey (2019) on Rating Middle-Income Housing Affordability* stated that "Hong Kong has the least affordable housing for the ninth straight year" and

---

19th, 2019, https://www.scmp.com/news/hong-kong/health-environment/article/3006921/hong-kong-doctors-agree-exempt-foreign-trained.

[36] Radio Hong Kong, "Don't ease the way for foreign doctors: Pierre Chan," April 19th, 2019, https://news.rthk.hk/rthk/en/component/k2/1453628-20190419.htm.

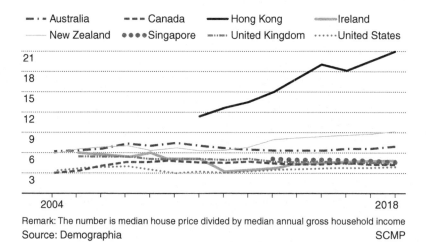

Figure 2. Housing affordability in Hong Kong and other places.

recorded the highest ever globally. CNBC posted a headline in 2019, "Hong Kong named the world's most expensive city to buy a home".[37] The graph in Figure 2 illustrates.

Shockingly, there was no matching increase in housing supply while the population surge took place. To start with, built up on land did not match demand. The Research Office of the Legislative Council Secretariat (ISSH04/2016-17) pointed out that in Hong Kong, only 24% of the land had been built up and only 7% was for residential use. Furthermore, Figure 2 in the report, which is reproduced as Figure 3, showed that there was too little incremental built up of accommodation between 2007 to 2015. The report stated, "*In Hong Kong, the pace of land creation has slowed down considerably in recent years. Between 2007–2009 and 2013–2015, the total area of built-up land increased by a mere 1000 hectares, significantly smaller than that in the preceding years.*" (The Chief Executive from 2005 to 2012 was Donald Tsang and

---

[37] CNBC, "Hong Kong named the world's most expensive city to buy a home," April 12th, 2019, https://www.cnbc.com/2019/04/12/hong-kong-average-house-price-hits-1point2-million.html.

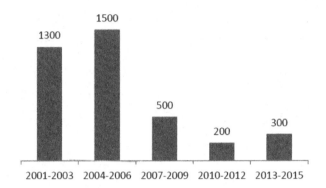

Figure 3. Increase in built-up land in hectares between 2001–2015.

from 2012 to 2017 was Chun-Ying Leung.)[38] The report mentioned land reclamation was a way to provide buildable land, which environmentalists objected to.

Furthermore, the provision of public housing fell behind. Amidst a large influx of immigrants reaching a million, public rental flats rose merely by 0.13 million units, from 0.67 million in 1997 to 0.8 million in 2017 Q1, as shown in Figure 4 below, which appeared in the South China Morning Post in February 2017.[39] In the same period, median public housing monthly rent rose relative more from HK$1,132 to HK$1,500 (33%) while private median monthly rent rose relative more from HK$6,500 to HK$10,000 (54%). The rise in median public housing rental did not outpace the growth in the minimum wage and was smaller than the period's HK per capita GDP growth (60% in the constant dollar).[40] Government-subsidised

---

[38] Chief Executive Leung commissioned a committee to study ways to increase housing supply.

[39] South China Morning Post, "Hong Kong's housing shortage is not one of needs but of aspirations," Opinion by Jake Van Der Kamp, February 7th, 2017, https://www.scmp.com/business/article/2132440/hong-kongs-housing-shortage-not-one-needs-aspirations. Data in this paragraph was extracted from Mr. Van Der Kamp's opinion piece.

[40] Hong Kong set up a minimum wage in 2011 at HK$28. It rose by 16% to HK$32.5 in 2015 and 2016. Some back of envelope calculation will show that the median rent for public rental housing kept pace with the salary of the lower income group.

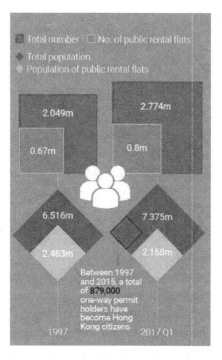

Total number ☐ No. of public rental flats
Total population
Population of public rental flats

2.049m

2.774m

0.67m

0.8m

6.516m

7.375m

2.463m

2.168m

Between 1997 and 2015, a total of 879,000 one-way permit holders have become Hong Kong citizens

1997

2017 Q1

Figure 4. Provision of public housing 1997 vs 2017.

rental units were then an increasingly attractive deal. Economics says that limited supply and low stipulated price results in huge excess demand and a long queue. Figure 5 (reproduced from August 8th, 2018, South China Morning Post) shows that in 2018, the average waiting time for a Hong Kong government housing flat reached 5 years and 3 months, almost reaching the previous high in 1997. There were 268,500 applicants, more than half (56%) were families and the rest were single non-elderly applicants. Many of the applicants were in the low-income group living in harsh conditions, dealing with the constant threat of expensive rent and forced relocation.[41] There were many sad stories which bred dissatisfied souls.

---

[41] South China Morning Post, "Waiting time for a Hong Kong public housing flat longest in 18 years: five years, three months," (Naomi Ng and Xinqi Su) August 10th, 2018,

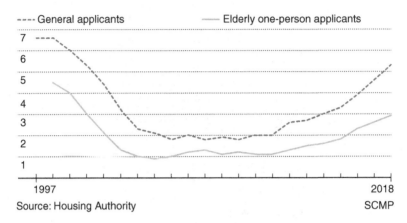

Figure 5. Average waiting time for public housing as of June every year.

In general, the provision of affordable housing in Hong Kong is severely lacking because of Hong Kong's "pro-market" economic policies. Here, a market structure problem rises. When left on their own, developers facing a growing economy will naturally cater to developing land and structures with high growth prospects and high-profit margin. This issue has been recognised everywhere in Asia. Take Singapore as an example, it has a systemic government scheme led by its Housing and Development Board since 1960. The Board was established by the People's Action Party, which has been the ruling majority party since Singapore gained full self-governance in 1959 and independence in 1965. Singaporeans' household homeownership rate has been about 90% since 2000 except in 2009, 2010, and 2011 when it was 88.8%, 87.2%, and 88.2% respectively. The British-HK government had made commendable efforts too — Home Ownership Scheme, Flat (of subsidised rental) for Sales, and even a homeownership scheme for the sandwiched class — from the 1950s to the 1990s, to promote government-supported development of affordable housing.[42] It installed rent

---

https://www.scmp.com/news/hong-kong/community/article/2159237/waiting-time-hong-kong-public-housing-flat-longest-18-years.

[42] David Faure (2003) *Colonialism and the Hong Kong Mentality*. The University of Hong Kong.

control since 1921 and passed an amendment bill in 1992 to allow rent to match the market price in 1994. Yet, it extended the timeline two times to 1998 clearly stating that it would be "inappropriate for the Government to allow rent control to lapse without any complementary measures to improve the rent-to-income ratio of tenants living in rent-controlled premises."[43]

The Hong Kong SAR government on the other hand, followed the non-intervention principle. It allowed rent control to lapse in 1998, probably thinking that economic incentives could induce supply. The government did not blindly apply economic incentives. The first Chief Executive Tung Chee-Hwa, seeing an acute shortage of affordable housing, proposed as one of his administrative agendas in 1997 to provide 85,000 low-cost flats to the market. Unfortunately, the Asian Financial Crisis plummeted property prices. The plan was shelved within a year under the pressure of public opinion about what the added supply would do to property prices. The Legislative Council pressed down the proposal; the government was not able to increase land and housing supply.[44]

Clearly, something was not right. Why was the plan not proposed again? Short-term cyclicality should not be the key consideration in carrying out long-term policies. Given the plan was long-term in nature, the government could just have delayed the plan for a year or so. Moreover, anyone with an understanding of demand and supply, and an appreciation of long-term population and economic growth, could be convinced over time. The building of affordable flats was for meeting a huge increase in demand at the lower end of the market. While that would somewhat mitigate the price in the lower end of private flats, doing so would not dent developers' profit margins too much, while not

---

[43] Section 5 of "Information Note: Tenancy Control in Selected Places," Research Office, Legislative Council Secretariat of Hong Kong, IN16-16-17, July 2017.

[44] South China Morning Post, "No Hong Kong housing crisis if ex-leader Tung Chee-hwa had stuck to goal of 85,000 flats a year, Leung Chun-ying says," (Xinqi Su) June 13th, 2018. The article quoted the future Chief Executive, Chun-Ying Leung's comment on the "85,000 flats" proposal: "However under the pressure of public opinion, especially the Opposition bloc in the Legislative Council, we couldn't continue our push."

doing so would almost certainly bring long-term social costs. The Legislative Council, influenced by the Opposition, turned against the lower-income class without homeownership, many of whom were immigrants, for the interest of those with homeownership, Hong Kong dwellers who had already settled in Hong Kong earlier. (Recall that the Opposition was pro-immigration in the earlier years after the 1997 handover. The camp conveniently changed its policy stance causing policy inconsistency.) Inexplicably, the Hong Kong government did not raise the topic again until twelve years later in 2012.[45]

Chasing market value can go too far; the Executive Branch's persistent adherence to the practice of the non-intervention principle could and did backfire. Tellingly, Figure 6 below shows that the private sector housing supply has fallen short of government projection since 2011,

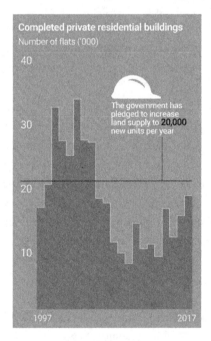

Figure 6. New houses completed, 1997–2017.

---

[45] It set up a steering committee to review long-term strategies for solving affordable housing issues. The committee recommended a 10-year plan to set targets for increasing the affordable housing supply.

Table 1. Major developers' land bank in Hong Kong (2017).

Developer	Land mark (sq feet)
CK Asset	6 millon
Sun Hung Kai Properties	21.4 millon
Henderson Land Development	14 millon
New World Development	11.97 millon*

Source: Annual reports *2018 annual report SCMP.
Waiting time for a Hong Kong public housing flat longest in 18 years: five years, three months
https://www.scmp.com/news/hong-kong/community/article/2159237/ waiting-time-hong-kong-public-housing-flat-longest-18-years
Published: 9:00pm, 10 Aug, 2018

three years after abolishing rent control. It is well known that a few big developers dominate Hong Kong's property market. It is also well known that they hog land: major developers hoard no less than 1,000 hectares of land.[46] This is very significant as the total amount of new land lease in Hong Kong is limited to 50 hectares a year by the 1984 Sino-British Joint Declaration. Is land-hoarding in a city known for shortage in built-up land a blatantly obvious rent-seeking monopolist behaviour (See Table 1)?

Hong Kong developers appeared to have a ring-bidding habit in government land lease auctions. They could even walk around the auction venue during an auction, perhaps to coordinate bids. Other than a 2008 regulation that forbade such walking, it took the government until 2018 to talk about developing a more transparent bidding process. Ample accusatory mass media pieces pointed to cronyism between the government and the super-rich who took profits from the masses in many non-tradeable goods.[47] Some of the reports could well be very

---

[46] See https://www.thenational.ae/business/property/are-big-developers-holding-hong-kong-to-ransom-on-land-1.812624.

[47] See for example, https://www.timeout.com/hong-kong/blog/tycoons-the-men-who-rule-hong-kong-100416.

biased and based on anecdotes or just rumours. Furthermore, these might not have done the necessary re-balancing calculations, e.g., their impacts on wage and job creation. We do need detailed research to obtain reliable facts and estimates for counterfactuals.

Nevertheless, a close connection between government and big businesses, including dominant banks, has existed in Hong Kong since colonial times. There were rumours that the government then channelled major public projects to British interests. In this tradition, it would not be surprising that Chief Executive Tung Chee-Hwa granted a very important technology and development project (Cyberport) to Richard Li Tzar-kai's Pacific Century Group (Mr. Richard Li is Mr. Li Ka-Shing's second son) in 1999 without competitive bidding.[48] It also follows that powerful business people and corporations have just been following traditional practices; they have not broken any laws. They are businessmen, as tycoons might say.

Still, people are naturally against unfettered profit-seeking. Many modern-day economic studies show that economic power can turn into political power which facilitates economic entrenchment.[49] Hong Kong's low-income tax, zero tax on capital gains and dividends, and the zero inheritance tax (legislated in 2006), coupled with high property costs, translate to a very regressive and effective tax burden on the middle-income class. The middle-income group and those living from hand-to-mouth (yet not qualified for social assistance) are continually being squeezed.

Hong Kong is now in a different era. In colonial times, people had no representation. Now, there are elected members in the Legislative Council; they have the responsibility to represent the weak, as many political economists would predict. Chief Executive Tung was pressured to explain the 1999 decision by members of the Legislative

---

[48] South China Morning Post, "Tung faces Cyberport pressure" (Ambrose Leung and Dennis Eng) February 3rd, 2005, https://www.scmp.com/article/488047/tung-faces-cyberport-pressure.

[49] Randall Morck, Daniel Wolfenzon and Bernard Yeung (2005) "Corporate Governance, Economic Entrenchment, and Growth," *Journal of Economics Literature*; Acemoglu and Robinson (2012) "Why Nations Fail: The Origins of Power, Prosperity, and Poverty."

Council. Unlike their objection to the "85,000 flats" proposal, many economists may have taken sides with them. To be fair, some progress has been made: Hong Kong enacted its Competition Law in June 2012 and implemented it in 2015.[50] The question is how often and how effective legislators have mitigate poor policy-making. Furthermore, would legislators abuse their monitoring power and would that lead to the building up of bureaucracy?

While the legislators try to represent the weak, they have come up with conflicting policy directions. They often pick a convenient stance in opposing the establishment that gives them a short term in the spotlight. Do they really represent the under-privileged? For example, their stance for embracing more immigrants and their stance against raising the supply of affordable flats, while perhaps justifiable individually, are incompatible with each other. Moreover, their continuous pressure (e.g., requesting a judiciary review) on the Executive Branch based on "public opinion" creates among bureaucrats a blame avoidance sentiment. This creates an unwillingness to accept responsibility and to undertake any initiative to solve problems. Also, this leads to the creation of paperwork, and commissioning of expansive and time-consuming outside study reports, which outsources bureaucrats' responsibility. Allegedly, this has substantially delayed the time to get development projects approved and also raises the risks of building development. Normal business behaviour is that risks should be compensated with a greater profit margin, which contributes to an even slower supply of structure development.

The opposition legislators' behaviour is puzzling. Whom do they represent and what are their objectives? We address these critically important questions systematically in Chapter 7.

The very sad part of all these is that the hyper-active Legislative Council group acting as the Opposition incapacitates the Executive Branch to come up with a policy direction in preparing for the future. It may be that the Executive Branch is too used to following instead of

---

[50] See https://www.scmp.com/presented/business/topics/competition-ordinance-force/article/1890994/competition-law-starts-hong and https://globalcompliancenews.com/antitrust-and-competition/antitrust-and-competition-in-hong-kong/.

leading. Alternatively, it may be that Chief Executive Tung, who had tried to lead was brutalised by the Opposition and that made the subsequent Chief Executives hyper risk-averse. It could be that the super-rich, a combined force of both the developers and dominant players in the finance industry, have connections and can stop policies that may not favour them, as Profs. Rajan and Zingales describe in their book, *Saving Capitalism from Capitalists* (2003). Amidst all these, does anyone represent the people in need of affordable housing?

Changes in China

China's well-known rapid economic growth has immensely impacted the whole world. Since its economic reforms in 1978, China has evolved from a poor agricultural country to the world's manufacturing centre, the second-largest economy, and the world's largest exporter of goods. China's industrial structure has diversified and evolved from light manufacturing to now embracing physical and knowledge-capital-intensive industries. China's rise changes the industrial composition of many regions. Hong Kong is no exception; its economic opportunities have shifted accordingly. Hong Kong has a lot of adjustments to make.

In the 1980s, China looked up to Hong Kong for learning and as a window to the outside world. Hong Kong companies sent management and operation trainers to China while China sent trainees to Hong Kong as well. Companies began moving their manufacturing to China in the 1990s, especially as China's labour market developed. The pace picked up after China entered the WTO in 2001. Over the years, Hong Kong's manufacturing sector has all but relocated to China or ASEAN countries in Southeast Asia, it has less than 1% of GDP share in 2017 (4.6% in 2000).

Traditionally, Hong Kong was an important transportation centre for the China trade. The significance of trade-transportation has declined from its prime at 8% of HK's GDP to about 5% in 2017. Hong Kong's importance as a port continues to drop in ranking, overshadowed by growth in nearby locations like Singapore and Chinese cities like Shenzhen and Guangzhou. Still, it is prudent to expect that Hong Kong remains a very important port for international trade. Interestingly, though, Hong Kong's information and communications sector, the most-hyped sector in the 21st century, has not shown any change in significance in HK's economy, staying at 2.9% of GDP in 2000 and 3.3% in 2017.

Hong Kong's finance and insurance sector grew in significance, from 12.8% of GDP in 2000 to 20% in 2017. Its service composition has also changed; it is now an important finance window for Chinese corporations. For example, its Hang Seng index in 1997 used to comprise 6 British companies and 27 traditional local companies in utilities, finance, real estate, and trading and only two Mainland entities were included (CITIC and Guangdong Investment). Now, more than half of the 50 constituents of the Index are owned by Mainland Chinese and includes H shares, red chips, and private Chinese enterprises. Even for those that are not, their major business earnings are very tightly connected with China.

Thus, Hong Kong's economy has, over time, evolved from being a vital middle player in China's trade and investments with the rest of the world, to now being insignificant to China but for its role of finance. Indeed, Hong Kong's GDP dropped from being 27% of China's GDP in 1993 to 2.9% in 2017.[51] At the same time, Hong Kong's capable financial institutions, low income and corporate taxes, transparent business law, and generally its legal system attracted many Chinese state-owned and private corporations to bring direct investment into Hong Kong and list on the Hong Kong Stock Exchange (HKSE). Likewise, many well-to-do Chinese brought their wealth to Hong Kong to buy properties, to set up residence, and to get Hong Kong financial institutions to manage their overseas wealth, including those inside Hong Kong.

The current dominant industries in Hong Kong are real estate, finance & insurance, logistics, and retail & tourism, almost all of them are tightly connected with China. Other than retail & tourism, these sectors are all human-capital-intensive (real estate is very financial-dependent), and evolve towards

---

[51] See http://www.ejinsight.com/20170609-hk-versus-china-gdp-a-sobering-reality/.

winners taking more (which contributes to rising income inequality). There are two effects.

Firstly, Hong Kong being an open economy, sources human capital from around the world, especially graduates who understand the Chinese economy and are fluent in Mandarin. Chinese students studying abroad rose from 180,000 (81,227 in the US) in 2007–8 to 662,000 (363,349 in the US) in 2017–8. China internally graduated 8.2 million in 2017–8. In sheer numbers, Hong Kong youth face stiff competition on the market for human capital.[52]

Secondly, these human-capital-intensive industries skewed income distribution towards those with high human capital. Also skewed would be the ability to pay for real estate by both households and businesses. Hence, besides heightened accommodation costs, Hong Kong's business rental has also gone up. There could be a severe "market generated" rent extraction and downward pressure on labour-intensive jobs.

Thus, Hong Kong is now experiencing a hollowing out of domestic job opportunities and income distribution. Hong Kong's youth, including professionals, face stiffer competition on the job market than ever before, while job salaries and opportunities in the middle end up stagnant. Should they blame China for its economic growth? Indeed, around the world, scapegoating of China is trendy.

Unlike the rest of the world, Hong Kong has the advantage of building a close-range connection (beyond economic integration) with the Great Bay area. With its proximity to China, openness, and legal infrastructure, Hong Kong is naturally a favoured location to serve as China's financial center and to host headquarters of companies doing businesses in China. This natural and logical development will lead to economic integration and intimate connectivity. Hong Kong to China is like Manhattan to the US. As the US needs more of Manhattan's services, Manhattan will prosper and its cost of living will rise. People thus spread out to Queens, the Bronx, Brooklyn, New Jersey, and Connecticut; they work in Manhattan but live outside, and the whole

---

[52] Hong Kong universities recruited top students from the Mainland in the past. Anecdotes suggest that they out-perform most HK students, perhaps by admission selection.

larger region gains. The rise of China elevates Hong Kong's economic gains, but Hong Kong has to adopt direct-connectivity with neighbourhood locations in Guangdong. The older generations of Hong Kong residents likely view China's achievements since 1978 positively and many have opted to retire in Southern Canton (Guangdong). Many families now live on the Mainland and commute to Hong Kong daily to work. Some manage to move to the Mainland.

Unfortunately, the Opposition has been playing an anti-China-anti-integration strategy in every way they can. For example, they would object to measures that facilitate unhindered human and traffic flows, in the name of preserving Hong Kong's autonomy. In Aug 2020, some of them objected to China's healthcare professionals coming to Hong Kong to help fight the pandemic, on the grounds that China and Hong Kong had different professional standards. There perhaps could be a compromise. Regrettably, the running of a tug of war between two contradictory directions (open market vs anti-integration) leaves the younger generation alone to face a hollowing out of local opportunities and polarised income distribution. They have a lot of grief. Whom can they hold responsible for this mess?

Summary

Since the 1997 handover, Hong Kongers have been running Hong Kong presumably within the "one country, two systems" guideline. "One country" refers to Hong Kong being an inalienable part of China. "Two-systems" means that China has its socialist system while Hong Kong maintains its own capitalist and legal system. In practice, preserving "two-systems" means both China and Hong Kong respect and follow the Basic Law. The Basic Law has liberated Hong Kong from its colonial system and established in Hong Kong an opposition politics with balanced power. The system is foreign to Hong Kong's politicians — the Legislative Council is highly empowered; it is no longer run by an appointed Governor accountable only to the government which appoints him; on the contrary, it has the means to force the resignation of the Chief Executive.

In this context, Hong Kong has to engineer a path forward. Any plan has to accommodate integration with China, bearing in mind that in 2047 Beijing has the option to fully take over. The challenge is that this path — integrating a highly Westernised capitalist city, and its capitalist freedoms, into a huge socialist country more than two hundred times larger — is novel in human history. My assessment is that neither Chinese nor Hong Kong leaders at the time of reunification had a clear idea of what they were in for.

The power balance, as set up in the Basic Law, can lead to positive opposition politics — opposition can constructively constrain poor policymaking. However, this is dependent on the presence of a sound accountability system. Accountability is light if politicians are not held responsible for the consequences of the policies they advocate. This is Hong Kong's situation; Hong Kong is not ready for the democratic opposition system created by the Basic Law. Chapter 7 will expand on this critically important point.

Changes before 1997 has led to the formation of a devoted opposition core which distrusts China and also an increasingly suspicious social attitude towards fellow Chinese from the Mainland, e.g., the perception of them as welfare grabbers. The discordance can only be detrimental to Hong Kong's development. With light accountability, politicians pursue their self-interests and only pay lip service to serving Hong Kongers. In particular, given the pre-set discordance, they are unlikely to aim for developing a coherent Hong Kong amiable to the "one country, two systems" concept.

As a result, after 1997, the Hong Kong government developed internally inconsistent policies that desolated the less than privileged groups. Under pressure from the Opposition, Hong Kong duly took in a large number of immigrants from the Mainland and offered generous welfare support and universal hospital care. The influx of immigrants stressed Hong Kong's medical services and housing sector. The paradox is that the government, again driven by the Opposition, allowed professional organisations to restrict the expansion of the medical service workforce to keep up with demand. And, again, paradoxically, the Executive Branch in the name of practising free-market policies, and the Opposition in the name of protecting the value of homeowners' assets, each pushed its own preferred policies. They inadvertently collaborated to deprive the lower-income group of additional affordable housing while not constraining tycoons from extracting rent using their market power, thereby driving up housing costs for both businesses and households. Despite the apparent low-tax system, Hong Kong morphed into a regressive fiscal system inflicting pains onto the middle- and lower-income classes.

Externally, a fast-growing China absorbed Hong Kong's manufacturing jobs and enticed Hong Kong to become China's financial and business service centre; the movement was natural because of Hong Kong's advanced legal and regulatory institutions for finance and business and its high land and labour costs. Hong Kong's government embraced the change as it pursued the free-market principle. To serve the Chinese market, employers in finance and high-end service sectors sourced top talents from all over the world, including smart Chinese graduates from top universities in the US and Europe. Hong Kong thus attracted both Mainland investments and talents, further driving up Hong Kong's cost of living and competition for desirable jobs.

This strategy can be interpreted as letting Hong Kong and China play complementary roles — Hong Kong exercises its absolute and comparative advantage in serving China as Manhattan serving the US. The strategy is predicated on Hong Kong's direct connectivity with China, like Manhattan is integrated with the greater New York City and neighbouring counties (including counties of New York, New Jersey, Connecticut, and Pennsylvania). Without the integrative connectivity, lower pay Hong Kongers are stuck. Unfortunately, the Opposition blocks integrative connectivity with China in every way it can. Inexplicably, they place their energy on blocking pro-China policies, on blocking government policies, but not on helping the less fortunate.

Recently, the Opposition Camp, for its political objective, has threatened to vote against the passage of the 2020 budget which includes handouts to Hong Kongers struggling economically due to the Covid-19 pandemic. In the 2019–2020 session, the Opposition delayed the selection of the Chair of the Legislative Council House Committee for seven months. The House Committee makes preparations for Council meetings and considers matters relating to the business of the Council. Without the Chair and Deputy Chair, the House Committee cannot carry out its duties. Thus the Legislative Council cannot have its normal meetings. This has delayed 14 important bills that the Legislative Council has pending, ranging from the appointment of the Chief Justice to a bill on maternity leave.[53] The Legislative Council is dysfunctional, and Hong Kong is stuck. There is a Cantonese saying, "Hinder the globe from turning". The LegCo in Hong Kong is doing precisely that.

Clearly, there is a fundamental lack in accountability here. What is each camp doing? What is the effect of each camp's policy? Which camp should be responsible for the internally inconsistent and driftless economic and social policies that Hong Kong has had to endure? The Opposite practices cynical opposition; the Legislative Council is dysfunctional; and the Executive Branch has no will and leadership. They all should be held accountable for Hong Kong people's tremendous suffering.

---

[53] The political objective is to deny passing of a bill that adopts China's national anthem as Hong Kong's too. Readers who understand Cantonese can go to https://www.legco.gov.hk/yr19-20/english/hc/agenda/hc20191101.htm to listen to nineteen meetings with driftless discussions from October 2019 to May 2020. The meetings were chaired by Dennis Kwok.

Chapter 5

A Series of Protests Leading to the 2019–2020 Social Unrest

E conomic history reveals that since 1997 Hong Kong has experienced more than twenty years of a tug of war between the Opposition and the Executive Branch. Due to low accountability, politicians in opposite camps each pursue their political agendas. The previous chapter documents that they together generate a series of blatantly inconsistent and incoherent policies. Despite Hong Kong's decades of rapid per capita GDP growth, inconsistent government policies leave Hong Kong's less than privileged, particularly the younger generation, with enormous economic stress. They face sky-high housing costs and miserable living conditions, fierce competition for high-end jobs, and generally a hollowing-out economy. The younger generation feels helpless and is emotional.

Many societies similarly experience rapid adjustments to, e.g., a large flux of immigrants, fast technological progress, or globalisation. These changes generate gains for a few but high adjustment burdens for the rest, especially for the poor and young. As the inequality intensifies, a little incident can trigger widespread protests. In France, an increase in fuel tax purported to combat global warming triggered the yellow vest protest in 2018; it quickly became a massive social unrest mobilising dissatisfied people from all walks of life.[54] In Chile, the increase in metro fares triggered a large scale student-led protest; the government declared a state of emergency and called in troops. In Lebanon, a 20-cent tax on WhatsApp calls as a part of the government's austerity policies to bring down a very high public debt burden triggered a mass "revolt" that lasted for five days in October 2019.[55]

An amendment to an existing extradition bill triggered Hong Kong's year-long unrest. How long-lasting and how violent it became surprised many Hong Kongers. Serious physical actions started on June 12th, 2019. I vividly remember a casual conversation I had in August 2019 with an editor of a very reputable English newspaper in Hong Kong; she felt shocked that the protesters (some call them rioters) had the energy and resources to sustain their actions for two months. Little did we know then that ten months later (June 2020) Hong Kong is still haunted by the on-going unrest.

Hong Kong's experiences could be a condensed and intensified version of how the masses reacts when the government, the market, and the society fail to adjust to changes in a way that balances the interests of multiple groups in the current and future generations. However, there are factors beyond just economic inequality. Several curious and vital questions will lead to deeper probing.

Firstly, the economic stresses in Hong Kong — the influx of immigrants, housing difficulties, skewed income distribution, and cronyism between the government and tycoons — are well known; Hong Kong had seen worse before. Between 1950 to 1972, Hong Kong's population grew by 2 million (from 1,974,000 to 3,974,000), then by another 2.33 million until 1997 (6.3 million). Figure 5 in Chapter 4 shows that the waiting time for a public housing unit was even

---

[54] Channel News Asia, "French police lockdown central Paris as Yellow Vests defy COVID-19," March 14th, 2020, https://www.channelnewsasia.com/news/world/french-police-lockdown-central-paris-as-yellow-vests-defy-covid-12538598.

[55] The Guardian, "Lebanon's mass revolt against corruption and poverty continues," October 19th, 2019, https://www.theguardian.com/world/2019/oct/20/lebanons-mass-revolt-against-corruption-and-poverty-continues.

longer before the 1997 handover than after. Hong Kong's Gini, a measure of income inequality, indeed grew by 0.8 from 4.8 in 1997 to 5.6 in 2018, but was only slightly above global standards (the US's Gini grew by 0.6 in the period). Hong Kong's corruption and cronyism were serious during the British-colonial period. The Colonial government catered explicitly to British commercial interests. Because of rampant corruption, the government had to establish the Independent Council Against Corruption in 1974 to clean up corruption in the Police Force and the Fire Department. These comparisons show that Hong Kong's economic stress may not be worse than before the handover. Why is the unrest this time so long-lasting and heated?

Second, evidence compiled in the past two chapters shows that the economic plight of the younger generation is driven by Hong Kong's internal political problem. Indeed, the Opposition Camp may be as responsible, or more, than other politicians. Yet, it claims the support of the younger generation and their electoral votes. This is inherently paradoxical. Why?

Third, while China's rise does change Hong Kong's economy, it generates a lot of positive spillovers to Hong Kong too, e.g., in the financial service industry, tourism, and international trade. However, the movement has a very loud anti-China tone, to the extent that some demonstrators (or rioters) explicitly show demand for independence and disown their Chinese identity. Why?

Fourth, the long stretch of unrest has caused Hong Kong colossal trouble, and yet the protesters (the yellow camp) appear to have quite a significant number of sympathisers. The movement is beyond comprehension from a practical perspective. Hong Kong is an inalienable part of China, anyone driving the movement knows that Hong Kong will not gain "independence" (and I doubt if that is the majority's wish). Indeed, the movement is likely to intensify China's inclination to exert more control in Hong Kong. Many remain sympathetic to the movement even though they recognize that the actions are intended to provoke China but will end up hurting Hong Kong's economy deeply. What has China done so that so many otherwise smart people are willing to provoke China even if they will pay a high price? Where does the intense negative sentiment come from?

These are serious puzzles. We build an understanding by digging into history. The social unrest did not begin in 2019. It is merely the continuation of many years of protests and rallies that have shaped the current narratives prevailing amongst the protesting camp and their sympathisers. In the remaining part of this chapter, we examine the past protests and the current unrest. In the next chapter, we examine the protesting camp's accusations against China.

The Drivers

Amazingly, Hong Kong almost has annual protest against CPC or its own government. Right after the June 4th, 1989 Tiananmen Square crackdown, Hong Kong had a very massive rally. It was peaceful and reflected that the majority of Hong Kong Chinese were upset about how the CPC handled the event. After that, on every June 4th, thousands would hold a candlelight vigil in Victoria Park to commemorate the lost lives. The late Mr. Szeto Wah, a well-respected teacher and a former lawmaker, often led the alliance. Mr. Szeto Wah was a Hong Kong delegate in the Basic Law Drafting Committee who resigned after the sad crackdown. The rallies' theme has always been that the central government should release all dissidents, rehabilitate the 1989 pro-democracy movement, hold people accountable for the "massacre." Sometime some would go on to urge China to abandon the one-party political monopoly. These rallies built anti-CPC rhetoric — CPC was a one-party dictator which would use force to shut down movements for democracy and would not respect human rights.

The CPC has changed a lot over the years. However, it has not been open about the June 4th, 1989 crackdown. It would be hard to find any public discussion about June 4th, 1989. Some would suggest that it would be difficult to make a clear judgment on what China would be like without resorting to dramatic crackdowns to resist political changes in 1989. Years of fast growth since the CPC's 1992's relaunching of economic reforms are used as evidence that political stability brings economic development.[56] (However, nobody knows the counterfactuals.) Many on the Mainland observing the series of Hong Kong 2019–2020 riots may turn to this view, as they see the severe suffering in Hong Kong's economy (e.g., shop closures, unemployment) and the blatant display of violent nativism. However, some would argue that if CPC is confident that it has served China well, it ought not keep the event under wraps. Many in the world would want a proper treatment of this part of history.

Later, a group called the Civil Human Rights Front (CHRF) was formed in September 2002. It organises an annual protest rally on July 1st every year in Hong Kong's Victory Park; July 1st is the anniversary of the handover of Hong Kong back to China.[57] CHRF

---

[56] But one-party political monopoly is neither a necessary nor sufficient condition for political stability.

[57] Internet search shows a breakdown of CHRF's membership: Student Christian Movement of Hong Kong, Hong Kong Journalists Association, Hong Kong Council of the Church of Christ in China, Civic Party, Power for Democracy, Democratic Party, Pioneer Group, Asia Monitor Resource Centre, League of Social Democrats, Hong Kong Human Rights Monitor, Hong Kong Human Rights Commission, The Chinese University of Hong Kong Student Union, Justice and Peace Commission of the H.K. Catholic Diocese, Hong Kong Catholic Commission For Labour Affairs, Hong Kong Alliance in Support of Patriotic Democratic Movements in China, Hong Kong Democratic Development Network, Hong Kong Social Workers' General Union, Hong Kong Informal Education Research Centre, Hong Kong Christian Institute, Hong Kong Women Christian Council, Hong Kong Professional Teachers' Union, Unison, Hong Kong Confederation of Trade Unions, Christians for Hong Kong Society, Rainbow Action, Sham Shui Po Community Association, Zi Teng (紫藤) (an organisation that serves sex workers, especially those from the Mainland and Hong Kong), Neighbourhood and Workers' Service Centre, New World First Bus Company Staff Union, Association for the Advancement of Feminism, Kwai Chung Estate Christian Basic Community, People Planning In Action, Neo Democrats, Labour Party, Joint Office of Councillors Au Nok-hin & Lo Kin-hei, iDemocracy Asia, Cross Border Children Concern Coalition, League in Defense of Hong Kong's Freedoms, Leung Kwok-hung Legislative Council Member's Office, April Fifth Action (四五行動), Hong Kong Association for Democracy and People's Livelihood, Hong Kong Women Workers' Association (香港婦女勞工協會), 中國民主聯合陣線香港分部, 草根文化中心, 香港性學會, 香港女同盟會, 居港權大學, 岑永根社區服務處.

is a collection of organisations including groups that explicitly claim a "pro-human rights" and "pro-democracy" stance, or an "anti-communism" stance. Its members comprise religious groups, social worker groups, teacher unions, labour unions, the journalist association, Chinese University Student Union, LBGT, women's groups, and political parties. They have gravitated together because of a National Security Bill introduced in 2003. Article 23 of the Basic Law requires Hong Kong legislators to set up such a bill. Many members of the CHRF believe that, in the name of National Security, CPC will restrict their rights, will limit the scope of their activities, and may even declare them illegal.[58] Because of the rally, the Bill lost Legislative Council members' support and was subsequently withdrawn. That CPC has not forced the Hong Kong government to take action against CHRF illustrates that CPC works within the Basic Law, e.g., following Article 27 which guarantees Hong Kong freedom of speech, association, etc. We should note further that British-Hong Kong in the past had a strict Sedition Ordinance which was consolidated into the Crime Ordinance in 1972.[59]

---

[58] Article 105, Paragraph 2, 1997 Criminal Code of the People's Republic of China (translated) states that, "*Anyone who uses rumor, slander or other means to encourage subversion of the political power of the State or to overthrow the socialist system, shall be sentenced to fixed-term imprisonment of not more than five years. However, the ringleaders and anyone whose crime is monstrous shall be sentenced to fixed-term imprisonment of not less than five years.*" Note that a Sedition Ordinance had existed in Hong Kong since 1970, which was subsequently consolidated into the Crime Ordinance in 1972.

[59] According to the Crime Ordinance, a seditious intention is an intention to bring into hatred or contempt or to excite disaffection against a person of government, to excite inhabitants of Hong Kong to attempt to procure the alteration, otherwise than by lawful means, of any other matter in Hong Kong as by law established, to bring into hatred or contempt or to excite disaffection against the administration of justice in Hong Kong, to raise discontent or disaffection amongst inhabitants of Hong Kong, to promote feelings of ill-will and enmity between different classes of the population of Hong Kong, to incite persons to violence, or to counsel disobedience to law or to any lawful order.

The significant rallies before 2019 are as follows:

The CHRF organises political rallies almost every year since its inception.

2003 — The march opposed the establishment of the anti-subversion law as required in Hong Kong Basic Law Article 23 in the name of protecting freedom of speech. The government, attempting to pass the anti-subversion law, tabled the vote on July 9th, 2003. It backed down because Liberal Party members in the Executive Council withdrew their support of the bill after the July 1st, 2003 rally; there were then not enough positive votes to pass the bill.

2004 — The march was for *"striving for universal suffrage in '07 & '08 for the Chief Executive and Legislature respectively"*. The backdrop was that HK's government earlier asked the Standing Committee of China's National People's Congress for an "interpretation" of the Basic Law on whether universal suffrage could be implemented in the upcoming selection (2007) of the Chief Executive and Legislative Council members. This represented a departure from the initial way to make the selections, and interpretation of the Basic Law was necessary. On April 6th 2004, the Standing Committee (of the National People's Congress, China) rejected the request because the following was not met: *"the provisions in (Article 7 of Annex II and Article III of Annex III) for amendment (in selecting the Chief Executive and members of the Legislative Council) must be made with the endorsement of a two-thirds majority of all the members of the Legislative Council and the consent of the Chief Executive and shall be reported to the Standing Committee of the National People's Congress for approval"* [Basic Law Instrument 18]. That is, the HK government had not done its homework. But the Opposition blamed China!

2005 — Two protests were held, one on July 1st and one in December to *"oppose government collusion, and strive for universal suffrage."*

2006 — The march was to *"create hopes for universal suffrage and democracy with an equal and just Hong Kong."*

2007 — The march was to *"achieve universal suffrage and improve livelihoods."*

2010 — The march was for universal suffrage.

2011 — The march was against land hogging by real estate companies, against allowing women from the Chinese Mainland to give birth in Hong Kong, and against implementing patriotic education in school.

2012 — The march was against the widening wealth gap, tycoons and government cronyism, the influx of pregnant women from Mainland to give birth to babies in Hong Kong, patriotic education, and a continuation of the rally for universal suffrage. (The Hong Kong government subsequently limited Mainland mothers giving birth in Hong Kong. Hong Kong's Ministry of Education also withdrew "patriotic education" from school curriculums.)

2013 and 2014 — The marches in 2013 and 2014 focused on universal suffrage. In 2014, the Standing Committee (of the National People's Congress, China) did allow universal suffrage in 2017. The condition was that a nomination committee should be formed which comprise equal representation by Hong Kong's four sectors. (This in practice means a comprehensive representation of all Hong Kong people.) Also, each candidate needs half of the nomination committee's support to qualify for the ballot. (Instruments 24 and 25). The Pro-Democracy camp managed to orchestrate a Legislative Council rejection of the proposed solution. Then, Benny Tai Yiu-ting at The University of Hong Kong, Chan Kin-man at The Chinese University of Hong Kong, and Baptist minister Reverend Chu Yiu-ming floated the idea of Occupying Central in 2013 which took place from 26 September to 15 December 2014.

These rallies, which have lasted for more than a decade, have bred an anti-government, anti-CPC, anti-Chinese social sentiment. The establishment and the government have been labelled as practising cronyism. The Chinese government has been accused of wanting to suppress Hong Kong's freedoms, and Chinese immigrants have been marked as resource grabbers.

Experimental research shows that protest participants will socialise and be socialised. Once involved, e.g., with the Occupying Central

Movement, they continue to participate in subsequent protests independent of their original political stance.[60] People marching along for one and a half decades have been socialised to feel that they have to fight against the Executive Branch government in Hong Kong and the CPC. The participants' behaviour is no longer a reasoned reaction to perceived injustice, but a conditioned reaction to narratives and rhetoric.

There was a prelude to the 2019–2020 unrest: the February 9–10th, 2016 Mong Kok riot. Many unlicensed hawker stalls clustered around Mong Kok selling fishballs and other types of food on the first few days of the Lunar New Year. They typically drew some complaints. It was unclear if in 2016 the complaints were particularly numerous. Somehow, on February 9th, 2016, the second day of the Lunar New Year, the Food and Environmental Hygiene Department patrolled Mong Kok. (Hawker control patrol rarely conducts patrol during the Lunar New Year.) The patrol was peaceful and led to no arrests However, some "people from a crowd" started to throw things at the patrolling Food and Environmental Hygiene Department officers. Some tried to push a cart full of boiling oil towards them. (Note that the hawkers in Mong Kok were not involved in these violent actions.) The police officers at the scene at the beginning were mainly traffic cops without riot gear. They were outnumbered and surrounded; an officer was pushed onto the ground and continuously assaulted. Another police officer fired two warning shots into the air. Hong Kong Indigenous, a local radical group that promotes HK independence, rallied members to the scene to join in the action. (According to the riot organiser, they rallied for additional participation after seeing police reinforcements arrived.) There was throwing of bricks and bottles at the police. Police back up came and they deployed pepper spray and tear gas. There were 124 injuries. The rioters accused the police of

---

[60] Leonardo Bursztyn, Davide Cantoni, David Y. Yang, Noam Yuchtman, Y. Jane Zhang (2019), "Persistent Political Engagement: Social Interactions and the Dynamics of Protest Movements" presented in NBER July 2019.

using excessive force. A riot instigator, Ray Wong Toi-yeung, a leader of HK Indigenous, jumped bail and is allegedly hiding in the UK, but the British government offered no comment on this.[61]

The conflagration — supposedly prompted by a hawker control patrol in Mong Kok — seemed vastly disproportionate to the issue itself. Then Chief Secretary Carrie Lam called this an unjustified riot. A commentator said *"Hong Kong Indigenous has gained popularity in recent years, in parallel with a growing desire to curb Beijing's rising influence."*[62]

The multiple years of rallies thus contributed to the manufacture of a political bomb waiting for detonation. The "Fishball Revolution" was a rehearsal for the 2019–20 unrest.

2019 Protest Movement

Protest against an amendment to the existing extradition bill

The 2019 protests had a life of their own. They evolved from early peaceful rallies against an amendment to Hong Kong's existing Extradition Bill (proposed in February 2019) to an anti-China, anti-Chinese, anti-government movement. They led to unthinkable violence and social disturbance. The year-long unrest dragged Hong Kong's economy to negative growth. It could be a black swan in geo-politics in the next few years.

Let me explain the amendment first. Hong Kong's existing extradition bill was established before 1997; it did not cover China or the

---

[61] South China Morning Post, "Where is Ray Wong, the alleged Mong Kok riot instigator? High Court issues arrest warrant after activist fails to report to police after German trip. Pro-Beijing media say he is in UK," December 1st, 2017, https://www.scmp.com/news/hong-kong/law-crime/article/2122520/where-ray-wong-alleged-mong-kok-riot-instigator.
[62] South China Morning Post, "Mong Kok riot: how Hong Kong's first night in the Year of the Monkey descended into mayhem," February 10th, 2016, https://www.scmp.com/news/hong-kong/article/1911341/mong-kok-riot-how-hong-kongs-first-night-year-monkey-descended-mayhem.

government of any other parts of PRC. In 2018, a Hong Kong man killed his Hong Kong girlfriend in Taiwan and escaped back to Hong Kong.[63] This was allegedly the Hong Kong government's reason for amending the bill *"so that the Hong Kong government can consider requests on extradition of criminal suspects from a government of any locations which include Mainland China, Taiwan, and Macau. The requests would be decided on a case-by-case basis by the Chief Executive. Several commercial offenses, such as tax evasion, were removed from the list of extraditable offenses. Hong Kong courts would have the final say whether to grant such extradition requests, and suspects accused of political and religious crimes would not be extradited. The government promised to only hand over fugitives for offenses carrying maximum sentences of at least seven years"*.[64] Mr. George Yeo, a highly respected ex-Minister from Singapore who was once Singapore's Foreign Affairs Minister, said in Singapore on January 17th, 2020, *"I did not find the proposed amendments to existing laws unreasonable. It did not seem right that one could commit rape or murder in China and find sanctuary in Hong Kong."*[65]

After the bill was proposed, "pro-democratic" Legislative Council members arranged a sit-in at the Council, expecting that the bill would eventually be passed because they would be outnumbered. The CHRF organised peaceful rallies against the bill on March 31st, April 28th, and June 9th, 2019.

Knowing that the Legislative Council would conduct the second reading of the bill in a full meeting on June 12th, 2019, CHRF

---

[63] The murder suspect was Chan Tong-kai and the victim was Poon Hiu-wing. Chan had supposedly sent a letter to Mrs Carrie Lam saying that he had "decided to surrender himself to Taiwan" after he was discharged from prison for using Poon Hiu-wing's credit card. Allegedly, Taiwan wanted an extradition, not a voluntary surrender, of the suspected murderer. See Channel News Asia, "Murder suspect who triggered Hong Kong protests is a 'free man' with 'free will': Carrie Lam," October 29th, 2019.

[64] Excerpt from BBC, "Hong Kong-China extradition plans explained," August 22nd, 2019.

[65] George Yeo, 24th Gordon Arthur Ransome Oration, Singapore, January 17th, 2020, "Human Solidarity in a Fragmenting World."

organised a rally on that day. However, apart from CHRF, an internet group known as LIHKG was already in existence. There were other internet groups too. They became platforms to organise protest activities, to issue march orders to "strike" and even to swear to use "death to stop the bill". In other words, this was an organised and funded campaign with a purpose, as we shall see.

Some banks and shops in the targeted rally district were closed on June 12th, 2019 for employee safety reasons. Might they have got some hints of what to come? The rally made it difficult for legislators to even enter the Legislative Council building. The Legislative Council declared at 11:00 am to postpone the bill's Second Reading indefinitely. Nevertheless, the rally continued! It turned violent: protesters in the mid-afternoon (between 3 and 4 pm) charged and broke through police barricades, forcing police to retreat to their headquarters. Riot police were deployed to disperse protesters at the Legislative Council building, allegedly using tear gas, rubber bullets, and bean-bags. The Policy Commissioner declared that day's protest a riot while the protesters countered that the police had used excessive force.

After the event, the protesters raised five "non-compromising" demands: (i) full withdrawal of the extradition bill, (ii) a commission of inquiry into alleged police brutality, (iii) retraction of the classification of protesters as rioters, (iv) amnesty for arrested protesters, and (v) resignation of the Chief Executive (another version of the fifth demand is "universal suffrage for the Chief Executive and all Legislative Council members).[66] Chief Executive Carrie Lam declared on June 15th, 2019 a pause on the amendment bill. On June 16th, the CHRF organised another rally demanding the withdrawal of the bill.

---

[66] The South China Morning Post reports on October 17th, 2019, Singapore's Prime Minister's comment on the matter when speaking at the Forbes Global CEO conference: "The five main demands of Hong Kong's anti-government protesters are intended to 'humiliate' the city's administration, and acceding to them is unlikely to solve the deep-seated issues linked to 'one country, two systems', if Hong Kong did not work within its mini-constitution, the Basic Law, it would be very difficult to imagine that the unique governance model in place since the city's return to Chinese rule in 1997 could last until 2047, when the system is meant to expire."

It claimed that 2 million people had participated, the police estimated the number to be 338,000. (Note that if each person takes up 1.5m² of space, 2 million people will occupy about 3 km² worth of space. The distance from Central to Causeway Bay is 5 km and the maximum road width 30 m. The road surface is then about 0.15 km². This simple calculation suggests that the police estimate is much more credible.) On June 21ˢᵗ and 24ᵗʰ, rallying protesters besieged the Police Headquarters. On July 1ˢᵗ, after a rather peaceful rally, some stormed the Legislative Council Complex. On July 9ᵗʰ, the Chief Executive declared that the bill was "dead" and withdrew the bill from the Legislative Council on September 3ʳᵈ, 2019.

Expanded objectives

The "movement" then escalated its goal, which could be the plan early on. A pattern evolved since mid-June — peaceful rallies would be followed by purposeful violence and destruction of properties. The protests are now a movement (some call it a revolution) with the blatant objective to be anti-CPC, anti-China, and to promote Hong Kong independence. The Chinese national flag was burned or stepped on multiple times. Chinese firms, banks, and even shops owned by people with pro-China and pro-government stances were regularly attacked and destroyed. There were many recorded incidents wherein people speaking in Mandarin or voicing anti-protest opinions were attacked. Protesters often hoisted British and American flags during their rallies.

The movement's tactics included crippling Hong Kong's economy to force the Hong Kong government to yield, lest Hong Kong has "nothing left" and China loses Hong Kong's economy too. (The term used in Cantonese is 攬炒, which means make all sides lose big.[67]) Protesters forced the shut-down of the airport for two days. Subway stations ticket booths were destroyed, railway stations and tracks were

---

[67] In Cantonese, "攬炒", is a term for a strategy in a popular card game in Hong Kong. When one holds a bad deck of cards, he could employ "攬炒" to make all other participants lose as much as or more than he does.

damaged and buses were burnt. Public transportation was forced to come to a halt multiple times. The protesters found many means, some very violent and dangerous, to stop road traffic. Besides crippling Hong Kong's transportation system, protesters openly declared that they would destroy ATMs and would want to create a run on banks.

The Executive Branch of the Hong Kong government has been incredibly weak and non-communicative. The Legislative Branch cannot be counted on to legislate laws to temporarily restore normalcy because the Opposition party is on the protesters' side and many are deeply involved in the movement. The Judiciary is allegedly lenient towards the prosecuted. However, we should respect judicial independence and refrain from making uninformed judgment. The police have become the only force trying to limit the damage and to maintain law and orders amidst the very frequent protests. They have thus become another of the protesters' targets; complaints against "police brutality" become a means to sustain the movement.

As mentioned, this movement has divided Hong Kongers broadly into two camps: yellow and blue. Each camp comprises campers with varying levels of conviction. The deep yellow campers believe strongly in the use of force. Their objectives include separating Hong Kong from China. The less convicted ones support the protesting youth whom they see as bravely venting their anger and standing up to an incompetent Hong Kong government supported by a suppressive Beijing government. The blue campers think the riots are being financed and orchestrated (even trained) by outside forces, a "colour revolution" to drag Hong Kong and China down. They see false prophets fooling and sacrificing young people as pawns for their private motives. They also think unscrupulous politicians are using the movement to generate votes for themselves.

Escalating violence, rumours, negative emotions, and more violence

The pattern of peaceful rallies followed by violence and property destruction has become a regular script. There is an escalation of emotions. Clearly, many parties are at fault. Nevertheless, the following is documented in "A Thematic Study by the IPCC (Independent Police Complaints Council) on the Public Order Events arising from the Fugitive Offenders Bill since June 2019 and the Police Actions in Response", p.37[68]:

"The messages and propaganda on the internet that continued to fuel violent protests:

(i) *Appealing and mobilising people to take part in protests and to resort to violence;*

(ii) *Sharing information to act in concert to assist the violent protesters in clashing with the Police;*

(iii) *Teaching people to make weapons, such as petrol bombs;*

(iv) *Disseminating untrue or unverified information;*

(v) *Attacking Government Offices;*

(vi) *Vandalising pro-Government corporations;*

(vii) *Tracking the movements of police officers on duty;*

(viii) *Doxing police officers and their family members; and*

(ix) *Inciting hatred against the Police."*

After seeing a few weeks of such unruly behaviour, some neutral observers, and even some sympathisers, began to adopt a different view as early as at the end of June 2019: "Are the protesters (many are at students' age) becoming child soldiers applying mob rules?"[69] Were the anti-China, anti-Chinese, and anti-Basic Law political objectives, now far away from stopping the amendment to the Extradition Bill, too blatant? Why would we agree?

Some took condemnable actions. On July 16th, 2019, a group of "white-shirted" men had a confrontation with protesters on a street in

---

[68] Independent Police Complaints Council, May 2020, https://hongkongfp.com/wp-content/uploads/2020/05/IPCC.pdf.

[69] South China Morning Post, "People power or mob rule? Hong Kong's young protesters risk bloodshed by blurring the line," June 25th, 2019, https://www.youtube.com/watch?v=w6UJNw6hcjs.

Yuen Long, the New Territories. The protesters vowed to return on July 21st to "reclaim" Yuen Long. On the night of 21st July, a group of "white-shirted" men holding canes and wooden bars waited for returning protesters after their protesting outing in Hong Kong. The two groups fought. The "white-shirted" group chased the "black-shirted" group to the Yuen Long MTR station around midnight. They attacked people dressed in black there. Forty-five were injured. Black was the protesters' custom colour. However, unaffiliated could have been dressed in black too. Some witnesses suggested that the men-in-white looked like gang members. Police were tardy in responding to calls for help even though they received information earlier about the gathering of "men-in-white." The police's excuse was that some people had deliberately jammed the emergency hotline, and pointed to the protesters' websites pleading in advance for supporters to act as such. Mr. Junius Ho, a member of the Legislation Council in the pro-establishment camp who represents the New Territory West district (which Yuen Long comes under), was videotaped shaking the hand of a white-shirted man. They appeared to know each other.[70] So far, the police have arrested 37 people, including some who have connections with organised crime.[71] This is an often-cited incident by the Opposition and the protesters as "police-gangster" collaboration to exercise brutality. The real picture remains murky.

The protesters continued their activities. They occupied Hong Kong Airport form July 26–27 forcing the cancellation of hundreds of flights, claiming a protest to preserve Hong Kong's democracy and freedom, including the strive for independence.

In August, there were frequent protests followed by a high level of violence. Hong Kong was very chaotic. On August 11th, a female

---

[70] South China Morning Post, "At least 45 injured as rod-wielding mob dressed in white rampages through Yuen Long MTR station, beating screaming protesters," July 22nd, 2019, https://www.scmp.com/news/hong-kong/law-and-crime/article/3019524/least-10-injured-baton-wielding-mob-suspected-triad.

[71] New York Times, "Six months of Hong Kong protests. How did we get here?," Aug 22nd, 2019.

protester was hurt and lost one of her eyes. The mass media at the beginning said she had been hurt by a bean-bag shot by police. Photos of her or models pretending to be her became symbols for police brutality. Unreliable circumstantial evidence, including possibly fabricated photos, suggested that she could have had been hurt by the police's shot or a slingshot by protesters themselves. (Her lawyer applied to the court to deny police access to the medical records about her injury. Her whereabouts remained a mystery.) Violence continued to escalate — both in actual actions and on social and online media like LIHKG.

On August 31st, 2019, Hong Kong police, in response to a call from MTR staff, went into the Prince Edward MTR station to stop rioters from destroying MTR station properties. Some were recorded on video changing out of their black clothes in order to pass off as regular pedestrians to avoid arrest. Police found rioters holding hammers and box cutters and they attacked the police. (The mass media rarely reports these photos.) Chaos erupted. The police used force, closed MTR station exits, and arrested 52 people. Protesters' websites posted stories that police had beat people up indiscriminately. A probationary ambulance officer estimated about 10 to 15 injuries and later revised it to 10 including 6 serious injuries. The documents on the injury figures, hospital information, and the police orders to send those who were hurt from Prince Edward to Lai Chi Kok stations — were accessed 15 times on September 3 and September 10. Legislative Council member Alvin Yeung, who belongs to the Opposition camp, revealed to the public a few days later that the number was revised down to 7 and serious injuries down to 3. There was no record of any death. A news report cited the Fire Services Department *"blast[ing] the leak of [the] document, calling it irresponsible and saying it will lead to more confusion and misunderstanding"*.[72] Indeed public confusion and misunderstanding ensued. There is now a rumour in Hong Kong that the police killed

---

[72] South China Morning Post, "Logbook for removal operation of injured protesters at Prince Edward MTR station had multiple changes made to it, document from Hong Kong fire services shows," September 17th, 2019, https://www.scmp.com/news/hong-kong/politics/article/3027738/logbook-removal-operation-injured-protesters-prince-edward.

three to six people and threw the dead bodies into the harbour. Yet, no one has reported any missing persons. However, the Opposition and the protesters proceeded to hold regular vigilance memorial services for the "dead" at the Prince Edward Station until recently.

Violence further escalated. Videos showing how to cut the neck of a person appeared online. On October 13th, 2019, a rioter cut a policeman's neck with a box-cutter causing a 5 cm-deep wound, exposing his neck vein and vocal cord. On November 11th, in Ma On Shan, in broad daylight, some protesters set Mr. Lee Chi Cheung on fire (28% burns) because he had complained that the protesters were not Chinese. Some protesters yelled back that they were Hong Kongers; one poured gasoline on Mr. Lee and another used a lighter to set Mr. Lee on fire. Hospitalised, Mr. Lee only regained consciousness on November 23rd. On November 13th, an off-duty 70-year-old contract street cleaner, Mr. Luo Changqing, together with a few others, voluntarily removed bricks left on the road by the rioters (after their brick-throwing riot events). Rioters hanging around threw a brick at him and knocked him unconscious. Mr. Luo passed away the following day.

In between, on November 8th, an HKUST student, Chow Tsz-lok, was participating in a violent protest when he fell from a parking lot in Tseung Kwan O. How that happened was unknown. Records showed that the policemen trying to break up the protest were more than a hundred meters away from him, but he was running back and forth on the upper deck of a parking lot. Could he be serving as a sentinel watching and reporting police movement from the deck to help the street level protesters? For a while, there was a rumour that he had been killed by the police.

On November 12th, a station sergeant shot a 21-year-old student in his abdomen. The policeman had been chasing a few protesters. But when he was about to leave, a masked protester in white had approached him, apparently in an attacking gesture. A newspaper video showed that the masked protester in white was holding him and two more were approaching him, even after he had drawn his weapon.[73] Afterwards,

---

[73] South China Morning Post, "Hong Kong protests: shot student remains in critical condition after surgery to remove right kidney, part of liver and bullet, as arguments rage

the shooting took place. The police said that the protesters could have been trying to grab the policeman's pistol.

From November 11th to 15th, rioters seized The Chinese University of Hong Kong and on November 17th to 29th The Hong Kong Polytechnic University's campus. Rioters seized the Chinese University because the campus has a bridge over the Tolo Highway which connects the New Territories to Kowloon-Hong Kong. Rioters threw heavy objects toward incoming traffic from the bridge over the Tolo Highway to break the traffic connection between the New Territories to Kowloon-Hong Kong. Rioters seized The Hong Kong Polytechnic University on November 17th, 2019 because the university's campus is right next to the entrance of the Cross-Harbour tunnel that connects Hong Kong and Kowloon. Rioters threw stones and petrol bombs at incoming traffic at the entrance of the Cross-Harbour tunnel to break the traffic connection between Hong Kong and Kowloon. The rioters made 10,000 petrol bombs, used catapults to launch petrol bombs, bricks, and chemical-filled bottles at the traffic and shot flaming arrows and javelins at the police. They took the bows and arrows and javelins from the universities' sports facilities, chemicals from labs and somehow managed to gather bottles and petroleum (from an on-campus gas-station) to make the numerous petrol bombs. Some of the chemicals and explosives are still missing; police continue to recover some when they search rioters' hideouts.

The movement had degenerated into extreme violence. Beyond the list of violent acts documented by IPCC and the above anecdotes, the yellow campers terrorised opposition. They doxed people who raised objections to their behaviour and advocated harming them and their families. They continued to harass and even destroy shops holding the opposite opinion. They applied the same scare tactics to harass voters who supported candidates they opposed to in the Urban Council election in 2019. They were practising terrorism.

---

over force used," , November 12th, 2019, https://www.scmp.com/news/hong-kong/law-and-crime/article/3037265/hong-kong-protests-shot-student-remains-critical.

The irony here is that these people advocating democracy and freedom are using violence to stop dissidents, yet feeling self-righteous about their actions. (Meanwhile, they complain against police brutality, which I shall elaborate in the next sub-section.) Is this what a revolution is about? Another question is: how big is this extremist dissident group? Does it represent the Hong Kong society's true sentiment? Is the group using violence to rewrite society's power hierarchy? Who has funded these costly organized actions?

That said, the blue camp did not behave like angels either. While they did not use violence, they employed degrading expressions and terms, such as calling the protesters "cockroaches" and leaders of the yellow camp "traitors". Verbal abuse is also a form of violence.

From the second quarter of 2019 to the first quarter of 2020, Hong Kongers lived in a city of weekly, or even daily protests. More than 9,000 were arrested and 41 percent of them were under 21 years old, many were current students. ***Furthermore, the objective of the master minders of the unrest has become clear: make Hong Kong ungovernable to force CPC to take over the governing of Hong Kong so that there is an excuse to mobilize international condemnation and boycotts. Hong Kong is their pawn!*** Ordinary Hong Kong people find that their beloved city has become a city of violence, rumours, negative emotions, and more violence.

Biased mass and social media, police brutality

The protest has turned into an outright campaign against China, against adopting any Chinese identity, and against the Basic Law. The Executive Branch is impotent. The Judiciary is lenient towards the so prosecuted. The Opposition camp in the Legislative Branch is explicitly siding with the movement. The protesters and the Opposition see that the police are trying to prevent protesters from disrupting law and order. They advance the narrative that Hong Kong practises police brutality, characteristic of an oppressive government. Strangely, a significant fraction of Hong Kongers remain quiet; some are sympathetic and some are silenced by the yellow camp's fear tactics. We shall go further into this later.

However, for the moment, we must consider this question: why is the mass media so biased in favour of the protest? The Western media continues to praise the protest but does not report much about the rioters' targeted destruction of shops and properties or the harming of unarmed people.

Hong Kong suddenly seems to have a high level of police brutality and a lot of accusations have been levelled against the police force. Yet, how adequate and detailed has the investigative reporting been? Take the story on August 11st, 2019 about the girl losing an eye "due to a policeman shooting bean-bags at protesters" as an example. The story fuelled a lot of emotions that led to an escalation of violence. The situation is puzzling. What has truly caused the injury? Why would the victim's lawyer go to court to stop the police from reading her medical records? What is there to hide? Does this not deserve further in-depth investigative reporting? Then, there were all the rumours about police killing, as reported above. There was a widely reported accusation that some policemen had gang-raped an arrested 16-year-old in a police station on September 27th, 2019 and the woman had an abortion on November 10th, 2019.[74] What has really happened behind all these accusations of police killing and rape? Are

---

[74] The allegedly "rape" case is curious. In January, the police said that the woman's allegations do not match up with the investigation result. (South China Morning Post, "Lawyers for Hong Kong teen who claims she was gang-raped by police accuse city's top cop of trying to undermine case," January 18th, 2020, https://www.scmp.com/news/hong-kong/law-and-crime/article/3046682/lawyers-hong-kong-teen-who-claims-she-was-gang-raped.) On May 13th, 2020, "The police said it was a false accusation, the woman was now a 'wanted person'." The force was planning to arrest her on suspicion of misleading officers. The Police Chief said that the person had "absconded" and suggested she had fled Hong Kong. The woman responded by revealing that the authorities had decided not to pursue her complaint any further. She criticised the force, saying it had failed to investigate her case "impartially, in strict confidentiality and with respect for my privacy and dignity." She did not reveal whether she was in Hong Kong. (South China Morning Post, "Hong Kong police chief tried to discredit me, says girl who accused officers of gang rape," May 13th, 2020, https://www.scmp.com/news/hong-kong/law-and-crime/article/3084254/hong-kong-police-chief-tried-discredit-me-says-girl.

these true stories or are they part of a smear campaign? (On July 27, 2020, South China Morning Post reported that the government prosecuted Mr. Poon Yung-wai for publishing four Facebook postings, under the alias "Kim Jong-un", between September 19 and 21 accusing police officers of committing heinous crimes at the San Uk Ling Holding Centre.) Why is investigative reporting missing, even after the validity of these stories has become highly suspicious?

Emotion arousing accusations, however, have been diligently reported in the media. Strangely, anyone who searches for the protesters' social discussion chat-groups can find (and realises that) the protesters manufactured biased pictures that tainted police reputation and sent these to the mass media, both local and foreign. Some of these "eye-pleasing" (to protesters) pictures duly showed up on social and mass media.

On the other hand, the mass media has taken the initiative to provide biased reports. Thus, police shooting was reported, but the sequence of events before the shooting was not covered. Photos about police kneeing someone arrested on the grounds appeared in newspapers, but why the police did that was not reported. Generally, the mass media rarely reported many of the attacks on police. This style of reporting leads to the presumption that HK police are indeed guilty of excessive use of force.

The bias readily appears in direct reporting. On May 25th, 2020, CNN, in an article titled, "Hong Kong protesters have promised a 'miracle' but China's National Security Law seems impossible to stop," reported that "*On Sunday it was not just the force police used — tear gas, baton charges, and water cannon against unarmed, most peaceful protesters — but also the speed at which they deployed it.*" However, even on the LIHKG website popular among protesters, posted statements were rather silent about "police use of force;" a comment even said that the police had practised a soft hand. Also, the protest was not peaceful at all. The protesters attacked police, set roadblocks, and bricks and bottles were thrown at them from neighbouring high-rises. It was widely circulated (since May 24th) in Hong Kong that the protesters had beaten up a lawyer (known to be "blue") who had been walking by. The protesters' behaviour startled a 51-year-old cleanser; she got a heart attack. Similarly, there was no report that in an earlier riot four people were approaching a policeman even after he drew his gun. One was already holding tight the policeman while the others were coming from multiple directions. They might be trying to grab the policeman's gun. Most mass media did not show or discuss this, but there were pictures all over the mass media, especially the Western ones, showing that the policeman shot a person. There was an incident that a person ran his motorcycle into a group of police with a pro-HK independence flag on the bike. He hurt four police. There was little discussion on the attack and the reports were all about he would be the first prosecuted by the new national security law. In general, the sequence of events leading to arrest were by-passed but subsequent police actions were covered.

This style of reporting leads to the presumption that HK police are indeed guilty of excessive use of force. People who watch Western and mainstay mass media and also see what has happened in the protests might believe that there is a conspiracy against China, Hong Kong police, and the Hong Kong government.

The new mindset in Hong Kong, at least according to the yellow camp, is that police are "guilty until proven innocent." This is an important narrative for the protesters, it sustains their spirit: they are fighting a worthy cause against police brutality, the symbol of suppression, even oppression! Their websites continue to post stories, many possibly fabricated. The mass media is more than helping to shape the police as "guilty," they are limiting the possibilities for them to be "proven innocent".

Furthermore, many in the protesting camp also dress up as reporters, some are even as young as twelve years old and labelled as "reporter-trainees." Many have legitimate reporter identity cards.[75] However, and interestingly, in a search of a rioter's home, police found hundreds of

---

[75] In Hong Kong, getting a reporter's identity card involves submitting a photo and paying a fee to become a member of the Journalist Association. The person can be a trainee reporter with a student identity card upon the endorsement of a HK Journal Association member. Alternatively, one can be an associate member by submitting a photocopy, or link, or a hardcopy of a published article with no specified qualifications. For more, see https://www.hkja.org.hk/en/membership/apply-membership-en/

yellow reporter jackets and reporter identity badges. Other yellow camp members pretend to be ordinary residents and bystanders. Some pretend to be medical assistants. They obstruct police work and often accuse the police of applying force on reporters, medical workers, and innocent bystanders. Police are frustrated. Often in the heated situations, whether deliberately or not, they may deal with real and fake bystanders, reporters, and medical assistants the same. In some cases, excessive use of force could happen too. The mass media snaps photos and reports observations that they manage to capture. However, they rarely expose the "fake agents." In this way, the mass media becomes the accomplice of the movement.

Why is this happening? Human beings process information based on our pre-existing views — that is confirmation bias. However, why are these supposed media professionals who should be seeking balanced perspectives producing such biased work? Have they deviated from their role to report facts as fully as possible? If so, why? Further examination is clearly necessary!

Social and online media play an incredible role. They are used as platforms for organisation, e.g., the LIHKG and other protesters' chat groups. Through social media, many accusations towards the police force can be circulated unchecked: murder, rape, raiding without warrants, orchestrating their own riots to justify their brutality. For example, circulated videos (which are likely fake) include policemen pretending to be rioters throwing petrol bombs, and voice and image of "witnesses" of police brutality or even police killing (unfounded). Indeed, right after Mr. Lee Chi Cheung was set ablaze, there was a video showing that this was just a stunt to hurt the protesters' image. Some social media feature comments from "ordinary citizens" suggesting that police, not protesters, are the cause of fear.

Perhaps most importantly, members of these social media groups post messages that keep the protesters' emotions inflamed by **spreading extreme accusations and hatred**. Rationality and prudence have no place in these groups. Once in the group, there is socialisation and peer pressure to believe, conform, and create one's own horror stories about police brutality and the like. It feels like a group hypnosis.

Make no mistake, the blue camp is similarly creating incredulous crazy videos to paint the protesters in a bad light. For example, there are some videos that show foreign experts training kid-soldiers in Hong Kong. Further description of some of these materials would be redundant. Both camps are behaving in the same manner. These social media groups are keeping Hong Kong divided and emotional!

Taking Stock

From an economic perspective, many Hong Kongers are experiencing strong dissatisfaction with their lives. Inconsistent government policies, driven by accountability light politics, tilt gains in growth towards the rich, hollow out the middle, and drive up the cost of living. Deeply frustrated, people have to vent their dissatisfaction, particularly the younger generation with a dim future outlook.

An amendment to the existing extradition bill provided the trigger; a large scale and enduring social unrest unfolded. The unrest caused enormous damage, with thousands arrested and about 40% of them under 21 years old, and almost a billion dollars of property damage. Some of these protesters feel a sense of accomplishment and a feeling of being in control, when they destroy properties, block roads, and stop public transportation services.[76] Some sincerely think they are freedom fighters.

While the movement in a broad context is a vociferous complaint about poor and inconsistent government policies, it has changed quickly and dramatically. By late June 2019, it was no longer about protesting against the extradition bill's amendment. It may not even be a social movement for kinder and more inclusive development policies. Rather, **it has now become an organised campaign built on an anti-CPC and anti-China narrative, and sustained itself with an anti-police brutality sentiment** (which some think police brutality is

---

[76] However, they really do not have a plan.

manufactured.) Ironically, the movement has resorted to a high level of violence. The objective of some of the master minds of the movement has become clear. They want to make Hong Kong ungovernable so that the CPC has to take over the Hong Kong government. This would trigger international condemnation and boycotts. In their minds, this is a way to take down the CPC. The deployed tactics will indeed damage Hong Kong's economy immensely. The younger generations would lose the most. **It is most curious why so many young people have accepted the mission sincerely.**

For months, Hong Kong people lived through very frequent disruptive activities every weekend and sometimes during weekdays. The unrest very negatively affected Hong Kong's tourism and retail businesses, which are the bread and butter of Hong Kong's small- and medium-sized enterprises and the livelihood of the lower-income class. The property damage and economic losses in Hong Kong were just enormous; repair bills amounted to almost a billion dollars. On May 4th, 2020, data showed that the one-two punches of the continuous unrest and the Covid-19 pandemic made a greater than 9% dent in Hong Kong's economy (year-on-year), the worst so far in Hong Kong's history. The unrest depleted cash flow for retail shops, and the pandemic performed the finishing act of forcing the closure of many shops. Unemployment (a new high of 4.2% in 9 years) and shop closures rose to all time high.

We need to be mindful that there are human lives behind the statistics. The following depiction would not be uncommon in Hong Kong today. A single mom lives with her four-year-old in Mong Kok in one of Hong Kong's infamous "Bond Rooms" — one with extremely thin wall-partitions in a sub-divided flat, sharing the kitchen and toilet with many other residents. Her husband, an unemployed construction worker, had run away early in 2019. She took up a part-time job as a waitress in an eatery in her neighbourhood, so that she could take care of her very young son. She lost her job late in September due to the unrest. She and her son have survived on borrowed money and the hope that they will be able to receive more help from the CSSA. The rumour is that CSSA would be cut (though this is unfounded). She has been hoping to get her job back after the pandemic. However, Mong Kok has been, since the beginning, a regular site for protests, often in the evening and at night. The unrest has resumed since May 9th, 2020. Sitting sadly in her 4 m² unit, hugging her hungry son, she feels hopeless and is thinking about committing suicide. She and her child are one of the numerous real casualties of the lose-lose (攬炒) strategy.

The politicians in the Opposition camp grab every chance to sway the mood to their favour and ignore the suffering they inflict on others. It is difficult to know what they are trying to achieve. One possibility is perhaps re-election so that they can get income as legislators or district council members. They may also want to amass more political power so that they can execute their version of policies, which according to them, will give Hong Kong more human rights and freedoms and set it farther apart from China. Yet, it is hard to imagine giving Hong Kong more rights and freedoms, as it is already getting more of them than most countries. It is hard to imagine that Hong Kong will ever be able to practise anti-Chinese nativism, given how dependent Hong Kong is on the Chinese Mainland in every aspect — economics, food, water, and more — and that Hong Kong is already an inalienable part of China in contractual terms. Over the years, the Opposition members have been consistently opposing China, the CPC, and the Executive Branch. Yet, they have not done anything constructive for ordinary people in Hong Kong. The policies they advocate oft-time retard Hong Kong's economic progress and fracture Hong Kong. Many of these politicians, however, are leading a very comfortable life living in luxury condominiums.

The Executive Branch's lack of response to this very prolonged social unrest is incredulous: it is neither crushing the protest, nor compromising with the protesters. Its lack of meaningful action adds to everyone's frustration, both in the Yellow and the Blue camps. The pro-establishment camp, in my opinion, has not offered constructive solutions. Accusing fingers — blaming the Opposition, blaming foreign influence, or blaming the mass media and teachers for tainting young peoples' minds — whether they are correct or not, aggravate rather than reduce social tension.

During the year-long unrest, Hong Kong is a vortex of cynicism, distrust, and discordance. The mass media and social media are hyperactive and biased (at both ends).[77] People are inundated with rumours, and exaggerated, biased, or even fake news, from both the Yellow and Blue camps, about the rioters, the police, the Hong Kong government, the Chinese government, and some foreign governments. Emotions are heated, facts are missing, and anxiety rules. Some young people have become self-righteous in justifying their behaviour, claiming a higher level of morality, a holier-than-thou attitude. Others have become suicidal.[78] Many more have simply withdrawn, feeling deeply distressed and painfully chosen to remain silent, but all agree that there is a lot of hatred going around in Hong Kong. Can Hong Kong be peaceful and lovable again?

---

[77] A journalist wrote on his Facebook page that international media coverage of the Hong Kong protests is wildly distorted, according to independent data researchers. In my opinion, this is only an impression in need of empirical validation even though some do feel that way. People on one side have the impression that the other side is doing the distortion to suit their opposing motives and that reporting is controlled in China.

[78] South China Morning Post, "Hong Kong extradition protests could trigger a mental health crisis, experts warn," July 4th 2019, reports that "*Three deaths that included suicide notes or other references to the current crisis have been recorded since the mass protests began last month.*"

Chapter 6

The Narrative: Is China Repressive?

As the previous chapter describes, while the 2019–2020 Hong Kong social unrest could well be grounded on economic grievances, it has become an anti-CPC movement. The unrest is initially organised by the CHRF, a coalition of groups that accuses the CPC of not respecting human rights and limiting their freedoms. CHRF has been pushing for an anti-CPC and anti-China agenda. Since 2003, it has organized many rallies focused on (i) striving for universal suffrage, (ii) objecting to an anti-subversion bill, (iii) maintaining freedom of speech, and (iv) rallying against some internal issues in Hong Kong. These rallies feed into the 2019–20 unrest.

The Opposition politicians, the CHRF, or broadly the anti-China coalition are tied together by the following narrative: China is being run by a suppressive CPC, it is repressing Hong Kong and bit by bit depriving Hong Kong of its freedoms and human rights. A good illustration is in the Cato Institute's Commentary: *"personal freedoms are increasingly under threat in Hong Kong. Frequently referred to as pro-democracy activists, Hong Kongers are, in fact, rising in the mass protests for both democracy and freedom."*[79]

Many in Hong Kong disagree with the narrative, but many others do; some actively participate in the unrest while others remain sympathetic and even offer supports. It is, therefore, pertinent to delve into the validity of the narrative and related allegations. This chapter reveals

[79] Cato Institute, "Hong Kong: Withstanding the Attack," (Tanja Porcnik) October 7th, 2019, https://www.cato.org/publications/commentary/hong-kong-withstanding-attack.

that these allegations are not valid at face value. Nevertheless, the Chinese government's behaviour does contribute to circumstantial evidence that fuels the narrative.

Did China Repress Hong Kong?

There are lots of allegations along this line. Are they valid?

Denied Hong Kong universal suffrage

Let us examine the allegation that China did not allow universal suffrage in Hong Kong. China indeed rejected Hong Kong Chief Executive Tung's request in 2004 for universal suffrage in 2007. The Standing Committee of China's NPC followed the Basic Law in considering the request. It did not grant the request because, as it stated in its response, the following was not met: *"the provisions in (Article 7 of Annex II and Article III of Annex III) for amendment (in selecting the Chief Executive and members of the Legislative Council) must be made with the endorsement of a two-thirds majority of all the members of the Legislative Council and the consent of the Chief Executive and shall be reported to the Standing Committee of the National People's Congress for approval."* In other words, the Standing Committee did not reject the request; rather, the Hong Kong government did not submit its request properly.

Another request was sent in 2014 for universal suffrage in 2017. In 2014, interpreting the Basic Law, the Standing Committee of NPC **offered** that Hong Kong could have universal suffrage starting in 2017. The response first pointed out, according to Article 45 of the Basic Law, *"The ultimate aim is the selection of the Chief Executive by universal suffrage upon nomination by a broadly representative nominating committee in accordance with democratic procedures."* Then, the Standing Committee stated that Hong Kong would be allowed universal suffrage in 2017 *"on the conditions that a nomination committee comprises of equal representation of HK's four sectors be formed and candidates need half of the committee's support"* (Instruments 23 and 24, dated August 2014). In other words, the Standing Committee interpreted the Basic Law according to its spirit and simply mandated representative democracy, a widely accepted practice around the world. There was no order on how the nomination committee would be selected other than that: (i) it must be representative of all of Hong Kong's sectors, and (ii) composed in line with the way the old Chief Executive Election Committee was formed. (Currently, Hong Kong's election committee has 1,200 members comprehensively representing all sectors.) The request meant that the nomination committee needed to have a balanced representation of the high variety of subgroups in Hong Kong. There was no order against a potential candidate campaigning for positive votes in the nomination committee (like running a primary). (See also paragraph 2 of Article 45, Article 7 of Annex I and Article III of Annex II in the Basic Law.) Hong Kong elites were engaged in a healthy discussion during the time.[80]

However, the Legislative Council rejected the option. Since then, there has been a continuous accusation that China is not following the Basic Law for it has disallowed universal suffrage in Hong Kong. In my opinion, this is a faulty accusation.

The Legislative Council exhibited chaotic behaviour. To reject the "response" from the Standing Committee of the NPC, the Legislative Council had to have two-third of the casted votes be "nay" and the total number of votes needed to meet the quorum. After stretched rounds of debate, a voting time came. Many in the Pro-establishment camp intended to vote to accept the response. However, 31 of them left the Legislative Council Chamber temporarily, allegedly with the mistaken belief that balloting would be adjourned until a leading Legislative Council member from the New Territories (Lau Wong-fat) could arrive to cast his yes vote; he was fighting traffic delays. Nine non-pro-democracy camp members somehow stayed inside, apparently due to miscommunication. The ballot continued. Twenty-seven pro-democracy members voted nay as intended. For the 9 who stayed, 1 pro-establishment camp member voted no, and the remaining 8 voted yes. The outcome

---

[80] South China Morning Post, "SCMP Debate: How could the chief executive nominating committee be more representative?" July 28th, 2014, https://www.scmp.com/comment/debates/article/1560575/scmp-debate-how-could-chief-executive-nominating-committee-be-more.

(28 no, 8 yes) meant that there was more than a two-thirds majority against the response and there were enough votes to meet the quorum. The Standing Committee's response was thus rejected.[81] The Legislative Council has apparently become even more dysfunctional over the years, especially in the 2019–2020 season.

The informed would be critical about the allegation that China denied Hong Kong Universal Suffrage. Let us stock-take three points. First, the Hong Kong Executive Branch did a poor procedural job. Second, the dysfunctional Legislative Council had its lion's share of responsibilities in failing to make Hong Kong's selection of the Chief Executive more open since 1997. Third, the Standing Committee of National People's Congress proposed a form of universal suffrage that follows the Basic Law and is not unreasonably restrictive; but the pro-democracy camp objected. Two conclusions follow. First, there is no denying that the CPC did not give the pro-democracy camp its version of universal suffrage. Second, by all standards, the allegation is a stretch of the truth and is politically blame-shifting. We shall expand on *Blame Narrative Politics* in the next chapter.

Hong Kong is losing its freedoms

There is also the accusation that China is suppressing human rights and freedom of speech in Hong Kong.[82] Basic Law Article 27 stipulates that "*Hong Kong residents shall have freedom of speech, of the press and of publication; freedom of association, of assembly, of procession and of demonstration; and the right and freedom to form and join trade unions,*

---

[81] See South China Morning Post, "Hong Kong reform package rejected as pro-Beijing camp walk out in 'miscommunication'. Pro-Beijing lawmakers left chamber to wait for colleague — leaving just eight of them to vote yes," June 19th, 2015, https://www.scmp.com/news/hong-kong/politics/article/1823398/hong-kong-political-reform-package-voted-down-legco-leaving.

[82] If the subject matter is on how China handles human rights and freedom of speech issues in China, the protests would take on a different nature: they would then be a movement in a part of China (which Hong Kong is) against China's current legal and political institutions.

and to strike.[83] China has been faithful to the article; Hong Kong has a lot more freedoms now than during colonial times. Even the Cato Institute, which is critical towards China, reported that Hong Kong's Individual Freedom in 2019 is among the world's top three.

Indeed, China has been faithful to the Basic Law even though Hong Kong has not. Undoubtedly, China is firmly against subversion activities. Basic Law Article 23 commits Hong Kong to establish a National Security Bill, which the Hong Kong government duly proposed in 2003. The proposal prompted the development of Hong Kong's CHRF in 2003, which organised a protest on the grounds that the bill would limit Hong Kongers' freedoms. Hong Kong's Legislative Branch failed to pass the bill in 2003. China did not directly intervene in keeping faith with the Basic Law. Seventeen years later, National People's Congress of China, on June 30th, 2020 passed a National Security Law tailor-made for Hong Kong. However, the actions still follow the Basic Law, especially Article 18. We shall further discuss this in the next chapter.

Another example is the manufactured fear regarding the proposed amendment to the extradition bill, which the previous chapter explains. The Opposition camp in the Legislative Council and the Opposition mass media promote the idea that passing of the amendment would subject many Hong Kongers to the threat of being extradited to China. Their reason is that China broadly defines what constitutes subversion activities and what constitutes the leaking of state secrets. The truth is that the extradition bill does not apply to many of these cases. In the amendment to the extradition bill, the Hong Kong government promises to only hand over fugitives for offenses carrying maximum sentences of at least seven years, and political and commercial crimes are excluded. In China, the sentence for instigating or financing subversive behaviour (carried out in China) is not more than five years. (For actual organisers, plotters, actors of subversion activities, the maximum sentence is ten or

---

[83] For example, it has not openly asked Hong Kong government to take negative actions against Apple Daily and its previous owner, who is openly anti-CPC.

more years.)[84] Hence, within China, as long as one's "subversive behaviour" does not go beyond "financing" or "instigating," the bill does not apply. Furthermore, any decision on granting an extradition request would reside in Hong Kong's independent court.

All these show that observable facts do not support the allegation that China is openly repressing Hong Kong's freedoms or taking away its autonomy.

What is the Source of the Allegation?

Perhaps, trying to support or refute the allegation is futile because more often than not people accept a political allegation based on impressions rather than logic. There have been four impressions creating movements since 1989.

First, a coalition of politicians and Hong Kongers already harbour deep distrust and a very negative impression of China's CPC. The Tiananmen Square Crackdown started the distrust, which was then deepened by the CPC's nullification of Chris Patten's reforms in the Legislative Council. This coalition has a hardened impression of a repressive CPC. It has been promoting a distrustful sentiment in Hong Kong since 1997.

Second, there is a severe break-down in communication in Hong Kong. Many people pre-judge without learning about facts and details. Perhaps, this is because there is too much fake news or that facts and circumstances are too hard to understand Alternatively, it may be because "under-informed" agents, including newspapers and social media, sway people's sentiments. It may also be because newspapers promote the negative narrative because of their training. Journalists trained in the Western tradition somehow have the attitude that they should have almost unbounded freedom of expression in reporting. Setting up any explicit restrictions to that freedom is akin to committing a cardinal sin, which they see authoritarian states around the world do.

Third, there are organisers behind the movement aiming for revolt against the CPC; their job is to sway many to believe in the narrative

---

[84] See *Criminal Law of the People's Republic of China, NPC 1997, Part II Special Provisions, Chapter I Crimes of Endangering National Security.*

and thus join them. Balanced analyses and presentation are not their concern. Over the years, they organised rallies against China, explicitly or implicitly, on the grounds that China's government did not give people freedoms, did not respect human rights, and so on. Many Hong Kongers in their twenties, thirties, or even forties grew up with these annual rallies. They were inculcated with a negative impression about China by the Opposition Coalition over many years. Exaggerated mass media stories, half-truth news, and fake news further stirred up emotions and blocked rational thinking. They could further create or twist their own stories and analytics to develop cognitive resonance. They have been passing their attitudes down to their younger generations. A large anti-CPC and anti-China crowd that occupies multiple age brackets is born.

Finally, many pro-China and pro-government factions suggest that anti-China interests in the US, Japan, Taiwan, and other places, are engaged in promoting the allegation that China has a repressive political regime. The anti-China movement coincides and intensifies with the recent US-China conflicts. Anti-communism has been a mainstream social concept in many Western countries. Many grew up hearing the line that communist countries deny people freedoms and human rights. Many Hollywood motion pictures do a lot of the talking. How this firm Western social belief affects Hong Kong's coalition of opposition is under-studied. Many observers submit that China, a communist country is the world's fastest-growing economy that has elevated the most out of poverty. However, this observation creates cognitive dissonance.[85] Firm believers of the Western social belief will have to find fault in CPC; they may find some.

Did China Add to the Sentiment that It is Repressive?

Despite multiple decades of unfettered socialisation of an anti-CPC sentiment, it is still puzzling why so many in Hong Kong accept the

---

[85] See, e.g, Leon Festinger. (1957). *A Theory of Cognitive Dissonance*. Stanford, CA: Stanford University Press.

narrative. Indeed, some have shockingly accepted the narrative to the extent that they would act against the interest of Hong Kong, their home, and China, even though they are Chinese. Maybe the narrative is not groundless. We should dig deeper. (This begs related questions on their national identity and their education. We shall turn to this point in the next chapter.)

Has China added to the impression that it is repressive? There are a few Hong Kong-related incidents that China's government and the CPC have to reflect upon.

First, there have been stories about people disappearing from Hong Kong, possibly abducted to the Mainland. For example, a Chinese billionaire, Xiao Jianhua, was last seen in Hong Kong's Four Seasons Hotel and then turned up on the Mainland.[86] (Hong Kong is an amazingly porous city. Many of the prosecuted during the unrest managed to jump bail and fled Hong Kong.) There was also the disappearance of five booksellers in December 2015 into China. A reputable newspaper reported that the incidents *"shocked Hong Kong, bringing into question the city's freedoms and the value of a Hong Kong-Mainland notification system"*. While all these cases could well have been legally conducted (Xiao's case is the most peculiar), *"the incident(s) raised fears for the city's autonomy and concerns over the potential loss of freedoms and the effectiveness of the notification mechanism, whereby Hong Kong and the Mainland notify each other if a resident of one is detained by the other. China likely has its legitimate reasons for doing this."*[87]

The puzzle is that China released all of these people except Xiao and bookseller Gui Minhai. Gui, who had a Swedish passport, was

---

[86] South China Morning Post, "Missing Chinese billionaire Xiao Jianhua 'last seen at Hong Kong's Four Seasons Hotel' before entering mainland," Jan 31ˢᵗ, 2017, https://www.scmp.com/news/china/policies-politics/article/2066744/missing-chinese-billionaire-xiao-jianhua-last-seen-hong; and "Disappearing Chinese billionaire Xiao Jianhua awaits day in court as flagship's assets sale stalls," May 29ᵗʰ 2018, https://www.scmp.com/news/china/economy/article/2148154/disappearing-chinese-billionaire-xiao-jianhua-awaits-day-court.

[87] South China Morning Post, December 29ᵗʰ, 2016 "One year on: Hong Kong bookseller saga leaves too many questions unanswered," https://www.scmp.com/news/hong-kong/politics/article/2058000/one-year-hong-kong-bookseller-saga-leaves-too-many-questions.

sentenced to 10 years imprisonment for *"illegally providing intelligence overseas"*.[88] Another bookseller, Lam Wing-Kee, after he was released from China and returned to Hong Kong, accused Chinese authorities of kidnapping, forcing him to sign a confession of crime, and wanting him to "keep an eye" on his book buyers. He admitted that he was given the right to live in Taipei; he exercised the option. Yet, another bookseller, Lee Po openly denied Lam's accusation. He is living with his wife in North Point, Hong Kong, going back and forth between Hong Kong and China often. The remaining two are leading regular lives and live in China (Cheung Chi Ping is in Dongguan and Lui Por in Shenzhen). Thus, while two out of the five appear to have "something" on their books, the others are set free. Lam's behaviour is most suspicious and could be material for spy and political conspiracy stories.

However, why would China let go of Lam if it indeed ruthlessly disregards human rights?[89] China has not been forthcoming about the whole event. It could have mismanaged the cases, it could have something to hide, and worse, it could be both incompetent and disrespectful of human rights and freedoms. In any case, China's bureaucrats have themselves to blame for people's unfavourable impressions because of incidents like these.

Second, in recent years, as China's economy has grown, China has weaponised its sizable market power as a significant buyer or seller. Internationally, many significant countries weaponise their economies for their political purposes. President Trump provides ample examples of how destructive such behaviour can be, domestically and globally. It erodes international trust and cooperation. It also damages the US' reputation and plants the seeds of further decline of the country.

---

[88] BBC, "Gui Minhai: Hong Kong bookseller gets 10 years jail," February 25th, 2020, https://www.bbc.com/news/world-asia-china-51624433.

[89] South China Morning Post, "One year on: Hong Kong bookseller saga leaves too many questions unanswered," December 29th, 2016, reports that: *"'I think the objective of the move is to purposely tighten freedom of speech in Hong Kong, and to a certain extent it has succeeded,' said Lam Wing-kee, the only one of the five Causeway Bay Books associates to speak about his kidnapping. The other four have stayed conspicuously silent."*

Note that only large significant countries can weaponise their economies; the strategy will have an effect only if the initiating country has market power. Weaponising market power is fundamentally a bullying act. While Chinese citizens may understand that China acts to protect its territorial integrity or to protest a foreign country's hostile military positioning, foreign communities may not necessarily understand or agree. China has conducted a string of such acts, e.g., boycotting Korea's Lotte, limiting rare earth exports to Japan, limiting tourist visits, blacklisting entertainers, etc., the list can be very long. Frequently weaponising its economy without tactful diplomatic engagements, especially when done assertively, can be very counterproductive. A commentary in the Japan Times headlined "China's weaponisation of trade: Beijing uses its economic muscle to punish countries that refuse to toe its line," illustrates the sentiment of those bullied.[90] They push back: bullying acts disrespect people's freedom of choice!

Third, CPC has created the impression that it would restrict discussion or even cover up its past mistakes. For example, the official position of the infamous great famine (1959–61) that killed 15 million people[91] was that bad weather and flood caused the famine. Many studies and affected people knew that it was due to poor government policies and a malfunctioning government incentive structure.[92] The disaster coincided with Mao's Great Leap Forward (1958–62) and the

---

[90] Japan Times, "China's weaponisation of trade: Beijing uses its economic muscle to punish countries that refuse to toe its line," July 28th, 2017, https://www.japantimes.co.jp/opinion/2017/07/28/commentary/world-commentary/chinas-weaponisation-trade/#.XsAeFMBS-M8.

[91] The number is from official statistics. The real number may be much higher.

[92] For example, the People's Commune flattened farm productivity and the government system led to overdrawing of produce from communities. There are many meaningful papers on the topic, see, e.g., Nancy Qian, Xin Meng, and Pierre Yared, (2015) "The Institutional Causes of Famine in China, 1959–61," *The Review of Economic Studies*, 82(4), pp. 1568–1611. Randall and Yeung (2018) have a rather complete, albeit brief, description of China's unfortunate economic policies from 1949 to 1978, the year it started its economic reform. See Randall Morck and Bernard Yeung (2018) "East Asian Financial and Economic Development," in Ross Levine and Thorsten Beck's *Handbook of Finance and Development*, Edward Elgar Publishing Ltd.

People's Commune rural governance system (1958–1983). Discussions of these disheartening CPC mistakes are light in classrooms. Discussions of the crackdown in Tiananmen Square on June 4th, 1989 remain taboo. There is a frustrating lack of transparency, and yet many people know something disastrously wrong happened while the government was at least partly responsible. Restrictions of discussions of public issues have also intensified in recent years. The level of frustration has been growing in recent years.

Fourth, in the current social media era, China applies intensive controls on social media. South China Morning Post (June 7th, 2020, Linda Lew) writes, *"Technology companies that run China's social media platforms employ thousands of content moderators as censors and develop algorithms to prevent anything sensitive from being published or to quickly remove it, while foreign websites and social media platforms such Twitter, YouTube and Facebook are blocked. [...] Also, in China access to the foreign online world is confined within the so-called 'Great Firewall', and everything from criticism of the government to pornography is censored."*[93] Other countries may have done something similar in different formats. However, the perception is that China's government is most controlling in this sphere. The younger generation is more active than most in social media. They cherish their online freedoms. Knowing the difference in social media control between China and the Western world, Hong Kong youth would conclude that the CPC limits their freedoms.

These all naturally lead to scary snapshot conclusions: CPC's organisation structure induces incompetence, bullies, and policies that disrespect people's freedoms, and a CPC-led government is untrustworthy. However, this should be emphasised: one cannot grasp the CPC government's characteristics and its contributions to China based on snapshots. Over-generalisation leads to unhealthy stereotyping. Unfortunately, the behaviour of various levels of governments in China gives critics rich fodder to attack China and the CPC.

---

[93] South China Morning Post, "Coronavirus pandemic shows global consequences of China's local censorship rules," (Linda Lew) June 7th, 2020, https://www.scmp.com/news/china/society/article/3087866/coronavirus-pandemic-shows-global-consequences-chinas-local.

At the macro level, China's CPC is inexplicably paranoid about its role in history. On balance, most would agree that the CPC has shepherded China to its achievement of modernisation, becoming the second most powerful economy globally and poised to become the first. Also, with China's rise in economic power and improvement in research and education, the CPC has restored China's dignity. The work is understandably still in progress. However, on balance, CPC should be proud and confident, without feeling paranoid and giving any glimpse of being insecure. The open admission of mistakes helps to heal; the nation and the Greater China areas could then be more unified for more enormous strides forward. Trusting people can earn people's trust!

At the micro-level, we recognise that China's policymakers are intelligent, but China has a huge and complicated government organisation. Given its size and complexity, what would forbid the super intelligent leaders' subordinates from doing something unintelligent, e.g., telling the leader what they think he wants to hear instead of what he should hear, or doing what they think will raise their chance for promotion instead of truly serving China? The possibility also arises that the lower-ranked officials may be over-zealous, instead of prudent, in executing policies. All of these may explain why China's external communication is broadcasted like it is for internal consumption. China's government often tends to create its own perception problem. This is especially the case now that it is not keeping a low profile, unlike during the time of Deng, Jiang, and Hu.

China is a big country. China has to be particularly wary about playing up the nationalistic narrative. The sentiments of 1.4 billion people are not to be taken lightly. Any playing up of a nationalistic narrative can easily get out of control. Would it be the case that such over-playing leads to international push back?

China Trapped in an Unfavourable Narrative

The 2019–20 social unrest in Hong Kong is a large-scale anti-China and anti-Hong Kong government movement mostly conducted by the younger generation. We have to admit that the youth have valid grievances because Hong Kong's economic policies have led to growth that benefits only the rich but hollows out opportunities in the middle. The youth are, however, holding onto the blame narrative that their grievances are due to a suppressive Beijing government.

A local Hong Kong movie speaks for this. In 2015, a fictional film with the title, "Ten Years," won the Best Film in the 35th Hong Kong Film Awards. The movie contains five fictional stories about the loss of human rights and freedoms in Hong Kong in 2025 as the Chinese government exerts its influence in Hong Kong. It depicts a death due to a hunger strike against a National Security Law (which Hong Kong did not yet have then). It fictionalises that the Hong Kong government, influenced by China's government, imposes a Mandarin requirement to marginalise taxi drivers who only speak Cantonese, Hong Kong's dialect. It features gangster-like Hong Kong police officers and kidnapping of innocent people by China's secret police. It also has a story about the Hong Kong government taking suppressive actions to gradually kill off a viable local egg farm industry (which does not exist). The movie ends with a quote from the bible, "It is an evil time. Seek good, and not evil, that you may live" (Amos 5:13–14).

A lot of distortionary propaganda, like in the movie, make the narrative appear real. The Opposition Coalition has contributed to the development of internally inconsistent policies that have led to the economic plight of the youth. Ironically, they stand firm confidently and self-righteously in fighting against a "repressive" China, without reflecting on how their policy stance hinders Hong Kong's policy development. Frustratingly, they are short on providing causal linkage between China's alleged "repressive behaviour" and Hong Kong's social issues. Instead, they promote the "CPC is repressive" (and thus damaging their future) narrative using fictional material like the movie, particularly to the younger people. When challenged, freedom of expression is their shield.

Whether the narrative is valid or not has become irrelevant over time. It is fully formed and has firmly become the adopted belief for many in the younger generation (and so has the narrative of police brutality in Hong Kong). The 2019–20 unrest and statements in, e.g.,

LIHKG illustrate the point. Unfortunately, neither China nor the pro-establishment has found a convincing way to tell their side of the story. They continue to merely give glory to China's economic growth, hard sell China's achievements in infrastructure development, raise an accusing finger towards the Opposition, or resort to boycotts or by-laws to ban what they do not like. Instead of debunking misconceptions, their behaviour corroborates the questionable narrative of a repressive China.

Chapter 7

Accountability-Light and Narrative Politics

C hanged from being a colony to PRC's Special Administrative Region in 1997, Hong Kong has much more autonomy than the British government had ever allowed. Still, embarking on this untrodden human journey (a capitalist city re-integrating with a communist motherland), Hong Kong needed intelligent and coherent policies to guide it through the transition. Unfortunately, it was tormented instead by what I refer to as **accountability-light politics,** which has run Hong Kong down into a declining rut. This chapter explores Hong Kong's journey from facing accountability-light politics to being gravely overcast by **blame narrative politics**. Hong Kong is at the brink of being non-governable. Hong Kong itself is destroying the concept of "one country, two systems"!

As Chapter 4 explains, the Basic Law introduces a subtle but important change in Hong Kong's political system. In the past, Hong Kong's governor was appointed by the British government; he led the Executive Branch and had sufficient control of the Legislative Council over which he presided. Strictly speaking (and risking over-simplification), the governor was accountable only to his appointor, and Hong Kong had an authoritarian system. After July 1st, 1997, the Basic Law sets up a fundamentally new system: it empowers the Legislative Council. Hong Kong now has opposition politics to the extent that the Legislative Council has the means to force the Chief Executive to resign.

The problem is that Hong Kong's politicians are neither experienced in dealing with the system nor does Hong Kong have the right mechanism to make politicians responsible for their actions. This is akin to a big bus with a newly fitted dual driver system negotiating a new windy road with no road map. The two drivers always want to steer the bus in opposite directions. *The bus is crashing now!* The continuous political tug of war leads to inconsistent policies that widen wealth disparity, drive the cost of living sky-high, and deplete economic opportunities for the less privileged. These are the causes of the protesting younger generation's grievances.

Chapter 5 explains how the social unrest triggered by an amendment to the existing extradition bill quickly morphed into a bona fide anti-government, anti-CPC, and anti-China movement. The uprising, however, is actually fuelled by an anti-China sentiment nurtured over decades of anti-China rallies. The sentiment is grounded on a blame narrative: China's CPC runs a suppressive regime that will take away Hong Kong's freedoms and future. The narrative is questionable; the sentiment is manufactured, but CPC is not blame-free.

Given the propagation of the blame narrative for decades followed by a full year of unrest, sometimes extremely violent, Hong Kong has become a vortex of misanthropy, distrust, and discordance. On one side are those who hold onto a blame narrative and advocate "breaking the law to achieve justice." On the other side, the government and many others do not act to preserve Hong Kong's governability. They are like deer in the headlights with no will to fix the problems they create.

We need to dig deep into the fundamental deficiencies in Hong Kong's politics and society to find solutions. These fundamental deficiencies are also present in multiple societies, hopefully, to a less extent. While Hong Kong's history is somewhat unique, Hong Kong's suffering from these deficiencies is a condensed and intensified version of what many other locations may experience. This chapter discusses the two fundamental flaws in Hong Kong's politics: accountability-light politics and narrative politics. The potent combination is destroying Hong Kong. The potent combination can destroy other states too.

Accountability-Light Opposition Politics
The Basic Law gives Hong Kong democracy

The Basic Law sets up a power balance between the Executive Branch and the Legislative Council. It offers a formula to empower Hong Kong residents. Thanks to the Basic Law, this is the first time Hong Kong has democracy, something that the British government deprived Hong Kong of since 1842.

The Executive Branch's budget and many legislations have to pass through the Legislative Council, which has means to force out the Chief Executive. The Chief Executive is selected by a selection committee, which comprises 1,200 members. The selection committee aims to be representative of Hong Kong's business community, professionals, residents, and its representatives in the National People's Congress in China. The selection committee members are elected to the office either by their functional constituencies or geographic constituencies.[94] In the same spirit, members of the Legislative Council are elected. The Council comprises 70 members, 35 elected within their functional constituency, and 35 elected within their geographic constituency.

This balance of power between the Executive Branch and the Legislative Branch is practised in many democratic countries, although the partial reliance on functional constituencies to garner representativeness is not common.[95] Nevertheless, balanced power and open debates within the Legislative Council can limit biased policymaking.

---

[94] The election committee comprises 1,200 members evenly representing four sectors — (i) industrial, commercial, and financial, (ii) professionals, (iii) labour, social services, religious and others, and (iv) members of the Legislative Council, District Councils, representatives of the native residents in the New Territories, and Hong Kong deputies to the National People's Congress and Hong Kong's representative to the National Committee of the Chinese People's Consultative Conference. In 1996, when the committee was first formed it had only 400 members, selected out of 5,789 candidates by a Preparation Committee, which had 94 Hong Kong appointees and 56 Mainland appointees. Later, membership was secured via election within one's constituency.

[95] Certainly, there would be complaints. However, one has to take into consideration voter informativeness at the beginning of Hong Kong's transition out of a colonial regime.

There is a reasonable formula for democracy in Hong Kong. (i) Members of the Legislative Council (LC) have to compete for their seats within their respective functional or geographic constituencies, which together leave few in Hong Kong unrepresented. (ii) LC members can constrain biased policies proposed by the Executive Branch and can reject legislation that can hurt their constituencies. (iii) LC members will not get re-elected if they do not serve their respective constituencies satisfactorily. (iv) The Executive Branch will refrain from proposing budgets or regulations that it knows outright the LC will not pass.

Needs a sound accountability system

This democracy formula ideally can serve the people of Hong Kong well. However, it breaks down when a sound accountability system does not exist.

Earlier chapters already illustrate some of the breakdowns. Chapter 4 shows that the Opposition rejected measures to slow down immigration inflow, which raised the demand for affordable housing. Yet, it also rejected ideas to increase the supply of subsidised affordable housing. The two "no's" aggravated housing pains in Hong Kong. The inconsistent behaviour stemmed from Legislative Council members catering to different groups in different council debates. At one point, they catered to families wanting subsidised family reunification. At another point, they catered to indigenous Hong Kong residents who already had their own flats and wanted to see house price inflation. Here is another example. The Opposition objected to setting up a co-location check-point to facilitate the operation of the Guangzhou-Shenzhen-Hong Kong express rail link. Such an arrangement exists in many places around the world, e.g., the setting up of an American check-point, together with the needed authorities, in the Edmonton Airport in Canada. The Opposition objected on the ground that this allowed China to impose its sovereign power on Hong Kong. They might sincerely think that they were doing the right thing. Nevertheless, many Hong Kong residents are grateful for the smooth operations of the rail link. Hong Kong's long-term economic development needs integrative connectivity with China.

In a system with accountability, Legislative Council members would be held responsible for their policy choices. For the moment, we cannot be sure.

Accountability in a system means that society has mature mechanisms to hold a politician responsible for the consequence of the policies they advocate. When accountability is light, significant problems arise; Hong Kong suffers from that. Lacking accountability, multiple factions of politicians pursue self-interests while shaping policymaking. In Hong Kong's case, this resulted in short-term oriented policies that could be inconsistent and harmful to the majority of Hong Kongers over time, as we have seen in Chapter 4. It also results in politicians using their position to pursue their preferred development with little regard for what people actually prefer. The world beware, Hong Kong is a clear example of how accountability-light politics drives "democracy tax."

Hong Kong's situation today is worse than what most could have anticipated in 1997. To start with, Hong Kong has a faction of politicians who harbour the wish of not being governed by Beijing. Some members of this coalition are in the powerful Legislative Council. Others include very senior retired civil servants, senior members of the teachers' union, and leaders in the CHRF, etc. Many of them are quite well to do and live in posh areas, e.g., the Peak and the Repulse Bay. The accountability-light political environment allows them to use their power as legislators to limit the development of pro-China policies and to promote anti-China policies, even if doing so harms the majority of Hong Kong people. Other members in their coalition not inside the government drum up "social support" for them.

An eco-system of accountability

Accountability is difficult to establish, especially in a complicated situation. Parliamentary arguments and debates usually have no external review. Facts come and go. Debaters use them opportunistically to create impressions and arouse emotions. Tracking the link between "actions and consequences" is a daunting exercise. That is especially so in Hong

Kong because it has unusually complex social-economic-political developmental challenges. On the one hand, Hong Kong has to adjust to a fast-rising China, including contemplating more integration with China. Hong Kong residents need to raise their understanding of China and Chinese citizens, both the ones living on the Mainland and also those newly migrated to Hong Kong. On the other hand, there is a desire to preserve Hong Kong's system; that is, its way of doing things. These are directly contradictory, more so the more vaguely Hong Kong's system is defined. Chapter 4 reveals that serving the latter can hinder the progress in the former. Promoting the former, however, can be seen as compromising the latter. The complexity and the delicacy in striking a balance make it hard to differentiate between those truly trying to serve the people of Hong Kong from those pursuing self-defined goals.

Still, other societies have their economic, social, and political complexities too. Modern democratic societies establish political accountability via (i) mass media investigative reporting, (ii) carefully conducted empirical and theoretical research subjected to a refereeing process, and (iii) political parties. For example, the US had the Watergate scandal uncovered by the Washington Post. Countries with a long history of democracy, e.g., the UK, the US, France, etc., have academics and think-tanks producing refereed in-depth policy analyses. While each report may still have some bias, collectively, they are quite balanced. Furthermore, political parties link an individual member's behaviour with party reputation. Thus, to protect its long-term reputation, a party will discipline the self-serving behaviour of its politicians. For example, the Republican Party in the US asked President Richard Nixon to resign over the Watergate scandal. Generally, a political party reins in its members to toe the party line and to preserve the party's reputation. Currently, many Republicans are worrying about the damage Donald Trump will do to the party in the long run.

Does Hong Kong have an accountability system?

Political accountability is based on a strong eco-system composed of the right capabilities and organisations. Did Hong Kong have that in 1997?

Hong Kong was at its infant state of democracy in 1997. The contextual background was that since the 1967 riots, Hong Kongers were apolitical, as described in Chapter 3. Hong Kong was a safe harbour to them. They preferred to make a living, not to disturb the political compromise between China and Britain. With this equilibrium and more than a century of colonialism as the backdrop, Hong Kong did not have the eco-system for establishing political accountability. The mass media previously had only a constrained form of freedom of speech, as discussed in Chapter 3, the section *"Liberalise the control of the mass media and broadcasting"*. Social science research in Hong Kong had yet to grow in volume and quality. For example, survey centres often used misleading questions to conduct surveys generating biased and unreliable polls. Political parties were just beginning to emerge. However, they were so numerous that it took an excel spreadsheet to connect who was with which party and which party stood for which political stance.

Accountability-light opposition and unrest

Within the accountability-light environment, Hong Kong had all the conditions that bred the explosive social unrest as Chapters 3 to 6 describe. The Pro-establishment and the Opposition camps were each pursuing policies they thought was righteous, or what they thought was right for Hong Kong. However, they did not pay much attention to a policy's consequences and Hong Kongers' real preference. Politicians advanced policies in the manner of catering to a specific group at a particular time, but they overlooked the incoherent and inconsistent nature of their policies over time. Alternatively, they just changed or withdrew policies whenever they faced engineered crowd pressure. The longitudinal connection between what they did and what Hong Kong experienced was not well documented.

Politicians tend not to admit mistakes. First, as described previously, arguments and debates made in parliamentary debates usually do not have to go through external review. Even if a fact check reveals inaccurate statements, Legislative Council members have the enhanced privilege of freedom of speech while in session. Most of the time, politicians only get punished by not getting votes again. Unfortunately, they would not get the punishment in an accountability-light system.

Furthermore, politicians have another weapon: the blame narrative, which is what Donald Trump has been deploying to deal with his poor management of the Covid-19 pandemic. We shall turn to that in the next section.

Here, it suffices to say that Hong Kong politicians' deployment of narrative politics, indeed, blame narrative politics, makes it difficult to develop the eco-system to provide accountability. It is a vicious cycle. Members in opposite camps are each promoting their interpretation of the "one country, two systems" and throwing blame at one another. In-depth investigative reporting by the mass media is lacking, because of the political climate, as Chapter 5 points out. Instead, the mass media, liberalised before the handover, becomes amplifiers of cynicism. Online and social media, which became prevalent later, is the conduit intensifying evidence-light blame narratives. Pretentious experts, e.g., academics with a poor record in refereed publications, became pseudo-experts misguiding Hong Kong's population. They exemplify "the Dunning-Kruger effect," after the research psychologists David Dunning and Justin Kruger, which posits that the less skilled are more confident of what they are advocating.

Blame narrative has turned Hong Kong into a vortex of cynicism and distrust, thus breeding the ensuing social unrest. The unrest in turn makes the development of a smart eco-system that fosters political accountability even harder. Politicians intensify their blame narratives. Hong Kong needs to break this vicious cycle.

Blame Narrative Politics

We now turn to blame narrative politics. Let us first refresh our understanding of the context.

The context and an illustration of building a blame narrative

Chapter 5 shows that the 2019 protest against an amendment to the existing extradition bill quickly morphed into an anti-China, anti-CPC, anti-government movement. Many who support the movement believe that the CPC is a repressive government breaking the promise of "one country, two systems" and chipping away at Hong Kong's freedoms and democracy.

However, the fact is that Hong Kong did not have democracy and had only limited freedoms during the colonial era. As Chapter 4 argues, "one country, two systems" is just a concept; it is the Basic Law that makes the concept concrete. "One country" indicates that Hong Kong is an inalienable part of China. "Two systems" means that China does not impose its socialist system in Hong Kong while Hong Kong runs the democratic government system defined in the Basic Law. (Chapters 3 and 4 explain this topic in details.) So, following the Basic Law is in keeping with the promise of "one country, two systems".

Chapter 6 shows that the evidence of China not following the Basic Law is flimsy. Rather, it is the Hong Kong government, including the Opposition, that has not followed the Basic Law. For example, it has not implemented Article 23. Also, legislators who openly advocate HK independence have violated Article 1.

Still, the Opposition, CHRF (the organiser of the protest rallies), the mass media (particularly the Western mass media) promote the narrative that young people in Hong Kong are fighting against the CPC to preserve their freedoms and democracy. As the movement drags on, these groups promote the additional narrative that there is police brutality in Hong Kong. Protestors have adopted these narratives to energise their movement.

A concerted effort to build the blame narrative is still on-going. On May 28th, 2020, China's Two Sessions (the National People's Congress and Chinese People's Political Consultative Conference (CPPCC)) passed a resolution designating the Standing Committee of the National People's Congress to draft a law, which would prohibit acts of secession, subversion, terrorism, and foreign interference that endanger national security.[96] The law can be added to Annex III of the Basic Law. The context is as follows. (i) Hong Kong protestors explicitly demand independence (in violation of Basic Law Article 1). (ii) The Opposition camp explicitly states it would want to gain control of the Legislative Council. After gaining control of the Council, the Opposition potentially can force the Chief Executive to resign and may even pursue secession. (iii) The Hong Kong government has failed to observe Article 23 of the Basic Law which stipulates that Hong Kong has to develop anti-subversion activities. (iv) Finally, the current Hong Kong government has shown that it is not able to maintain orderly behaviour in the Legislative Council, e.g., as demonstrated by the Dennis Kwok-led filibuster behaviour in the selection of the Chair of the House Committee (see the second last paragraph in Chapter 4).

Given these conditions, CPC's move is legitimate because **Article 18 of the Basic Law** stipulates that

> *"China's national laws shall not be applied in HK except for those listed in Annex III to the Basic Law. The laws listed therein shall be applied locally by way of promulgation or legislation by the Region. The Standing Committee of the National People's Congress **may add to or delete from the list of laws in Annex III** after consulting its Committee for the Basic Law of the Hong Kong Special Administrative Region and the government of the Region. Laws listed in Annex III to this Law shall be confined to those relating to defence and foreign affairs as well as other matters outside the limits of the autonomy of the Region as specified by this Law. In the event that the Standing Committee of the National People's Congress decides to declare a state of war, or, **by reason of turmoil within the Hong Kong Special Administrative Region which endangers national unity or security and is beyond the control of the government of the Region**, decides that the Region is in a state of*

---

[96] Channel News Asia, "China's parliament approves Hong Kong national security Bill," May 28th, 2020, https://www.channelnewsasia.com/news/asia/hong-kong-china-national-security-bill-pass-parliament-12779204.

emergency, **the Central People's Government may issue an order applying the relevant national laws in the Region.** *"*

On May 22nd, 2020, the South China Morning Post reported that

"Speaking at the opening of the annual session of the National People's Congress (NPC), Wang Chen, vice-chairman of the NPC's Standing Committee, confirmed that the law (to be specified) *would proscribe* **secessionist and subversive activity as well as foreign interference and terrorism in the city** *— all developments that had been troubling Beijing for some time, but most pressingly over the past year of increasingly violent anti-government protests. Wang said a fundamental consideration behind the resolution was that Beijing would not allow Hong Kong to be turned into a ba*se *of infiltration. [...] a resolution will authorise the standing committee to make relevant laws (which Wang Chen refers to above) to establish a sound legal system and enforcement mechanism for safeguarding national security in Hong Kong. The resolution also specified that Hong Kong must establish an organisation and enforcement mechanism to protect national security."*[97]

In essence, the CPC is following the Basic Law as defence against threats from secessionists and their acts of subversion, terrorism, and collusion with foreign interference. (Since March, the Hong Kong police have found many explosives and chemicals in various spots in Hong Kong, including in densely populated areas.) Note that Taiwan has established a very draconian and encompassing anti-infiltration law on December 30th, 2019.

The Opposition camp immediately reacted with the narrative that: *"China is practising 'one-country-one-system'"* and *"making such a law on Hong Kong's behalf without the direct participation of its people, legislature*

---

[97] South China Morning Post, "Two Sessions 2020: new law will 'prevent, frustrate and punish' acts in Hong Kong that threaten national security, top official says," May 22nd, 2020, https://www.scmp.com/news/hong-kong/politics/article/3085617/two-sessions-2020-national-security-law-hong-kong-will. The official announcement in Chinese is available at http://www.xinhuanet.com/politics/2020-05/22/c_1126019468.htm.

or judiciary would clearly undermine the principle of 'one country, two systems', under which Hong Kong is guaranteed a high degree of autonomy."[98] Some US Senators, as reported in a Guardian article, claimed this *"an unprecedented assault against Hong Kong's autonomy"* and saying that *"[t]he Chinese government is once again breaking its promises to the people of Hong Kong and the international community"*, making this *"an unprecedented assault against Hong Kong's autonomy"*.[99] Before the proposed national security law has even been written, CNN had already declared that it *"threatens the city's autonomy and civil liberties"*.[100] The Economist, in its May 30th, 2020 edition, featured a headline, *"Hong Kong's Freedoms Rule by Fear — The end of Hong Kong as a place with its own values and freedoms has been called many times. Could its time, at last, be up?"* The double standards in all these reports are troubling. First, Hong Kong is an inalienable part of China. Second, the plan to develop the National Security Law follows the Basic Law's prescribed conditions and procedures. Third, most countries have national security laws against treason and subversion — the US, Germany, and recently Spain. The UK had legislated numerous national security laws covering all of its territories, including autonomous regions such as Northern Ireland. In Hong Kong, it imposed a Sedition Ordinance and set up the secretive but feared Political Department inside its police force. The British government moved all documents and involved staff to England before exiting Hong Kong.

Beyond the double standards, the mass media propagates stretched storylines and exaggerates fears. Why would laws written by the CPC which are aimed at secession promoting subversive activities, terrorism, and resultant actions, be definite threats to autonomy

---

[98] South China Morning Post, "International opposition mounts against China's proposed security law for Hong Kong," May 23rd, 2020, https://www.scmp.com/news/hong-kong/article/3085744/international-opposition-mounts-against-chinas-proposed-security-law.

[99] The Guardian, "Hong Kong crisis: China presents security laws banning subversion and separatism," May 22nd, 2020, https://www.theguardian.com/world/2020/may/22/chinas-national-security-law-ban-subversion-and-separatism-hong-kong.

[100] CNN, "Hong Kong protest over proposed national security law met with tear gas," May 24th, 2020, https://lite.cnn.com/en/article/h_c1a520d00fbfcca24254c723ba0a4339.

and civil liberties while they are not so in other countries? Did the Hong Kong politicians in the Opposition camp who promoted the biased stories thoroughly check what the Basic Law (and Article 18) is about? And, did the journalists check the Basic Law before filing their reports? Why would following the Basic Law destroy the "one country, two systems" concept? Maybe some journalists and politicians are just following a blame narrative — the CPC will chip away at Hong Kong's freedoms. The exhibited behaviour collectively could create an impression that these journalists and politicians do not want a law in Hong Kong that prohibits activities they want to preserve. I dearly would not want to encourage such thinking.

All of these have sparked further protests. That the CPC has not yet (then) set up the new law is not the point, nor is it whether China follows the Basic Law. The accusatory narrative is. This is narrative politics at its worst. Facts and logics are irrelevant. Double standards are acceptable. An accusatory narrative that arouses anti-China emotions is reinforced. Hong Kong protesters are duly launching new rounds of social unrest. Simultaneously, those who believe in the narrative are sending multiple messages using social media, calling for people to come out to protest and also to foreign government agents and politicians for support. Western media will then write the corresponding news stories.

Humans use narrative

Human beings are hardwired to be curious and seek satisfaction of their curiosity. From birth, we observe and seek experiences. We ask "who, what, where, when, why, and how" questions to allow our observations and experience to "make sense" to us. Often, for what we do not understand, we make up stories to explain our observations and experiences. For example, our ancestors did not understand why the moon has shadows; they made up fairy tales about a lady living there. They did not understand why some people were more powerful and richer than others; they developed numerology, feng shui, and astrology to explain these observed realities. In short, as human beings, we develop stories for ourselves, to allow things to "make sense" to us.

Human beings are also inherently social. As social beings, we crave for the echo chamber effect in our communication with our social groups. We love to share stories, even fairy tales and ghost stories we know to be unfounded. We enjoy communicating on what we all have some knowledge of, we fill in each other's storylines and we then emotionally bond. Furthermore, a narrative helps to pass our concern to others by stimulating their concerns and emotions.

Some human beings especially crave rational logic, beyond just conditional reflexes. These people like to dig deep to obtain logically satisfactory answers to known questions. They become specialists. They develop competing and refined storylines, which become hypotheses. They empirically examine these storylines from multiple angles. There is a competition in advancing the most compelling hypotheses and credible empirical evidence to explain away intellectual puzzles. In the process, individual specialists practise "refusal to agree" — a refereeing process to separate the wheat from the chaff. Specialists also adopt the philosophical principle of Occam's razor — when there are two explanations for an occurrence, the simpler one which has fewer assumptions is better. And, these specialists ask further questions.

This is the process by which human beings develop science and knowledge, both physical and social sciences alike. People engaged in this process are scientists, or social scientists. These specialists make a living out of following the above process. It is a daunting endeavour, a scientist has to accept in the face criticism and the reality that in most scientific discussions, one's work is assumed defective until all criticisms can be rebutted and resolved. One has to particularly enjoy finding scientific facts and seeking truth from facts. Doing science is not everyone's cup of tea, nor is going through the excruciation process. Yet, being scientific is necessary for human progress.

However, the majority of human beings are non-specialists. Still, they crave to understand, and often, many living in the same society have similar questions. In particular, when facing complex issues, narratives are the recourse of non-experts; that is, ordinary people use narratives to answer questions on what influences our social experiences, lives, and society. Furthermore, we use narratives to guide our judgement on government policies.

In other words, a social narrative is a simple story connecting social players, phenomena, and feelings. Consider two storylines. First, my employer collaborates with the ruling class to ruthlessly exploit me by cutting my wages. Second, factors such as the progress in transportation technology, the rise in the neighbouring country's labour productivity, and global competition on product markets are collectively pressing down my wages unless I manage to raise my productivity. The former, relative to the latter, is a lot simpler and more appealing. Indeed, as described in the previous sub-section, the storyline that China is proscribing a national security law to "oppress Hong Kongers' freedoms and rights" (6 words) is a lot easier to communicate than China "follows the Basic Law to preserve the Basic Law, which is the meaning of "one country, two systems", and China has to do that because Hong Kong protesters are demanding the secession of HK from China" (36 words).

A social narrative has to connect with emotions. Hence, the Yellow campers like the 6-word version while the Blue campers like the 36-word version. Then, the narrative bonds with and reinforces existing emotions in the receiving group. Notice that there will be group self-selection: a narrative only travels within the group that it bonds with. The Blue camp says the 6-word version is groundless and the Yellow camp accuses the 36-word version of brain-washing. Narratives can be divisive!

However, all these will be alright if the narrative the majority adopts is rational and largely valid.

Narratives, thinking process, and crowd acceptance

Unlike experts, ordinary people validate narratives using casual observations and impressions, intuition, as well as instinct. If enough varieties of people make similar casual observations, narratives may be based on truth to some or even a large degree.

Yet, this is a very unreliable process leading to very biased and even irrational social development. (i) Causal observations can be biased. For example, a picture showing a policeman shooting a protester "confirms" police brutality, as long as very few pictures show that some protesters were attacking the policeman before the shooting happened. (The opposite bias develops if there are pictures showing protesters attacking the police but not too many showing the police kneeing an arrested protester.) (ii) If the same biased evidence, no matter how unreliable it is, is observed by many people, a narrative becomes a "firmed up truth" by the crowd. The advent of social media makes this a common occurrence. (iii) Human beings practise confirmation bias — we search for and accept what corroborates with our beliefs and tend to overlook or consciously ignore the opposite. Hence, people in the Yellow Camp will focus on other incomplete but similarly presented pictures to confirm police brutality. (People in the Blue Camp will focus on incomplete but similarly presented pictures about protesters' violent behaviour.) (iv) We can socialise others to adopt our belief because human beings are inherently social and crave for group acceptance. Thus, there is an escalating effect in group-based acceptance of a narrative. Visualise the following: a young man who participated in a recent rally acknowledges that the policeman who shot a protester was defending himself. The majority of the other protesters he is sitting with then accuse him of being brainwashed and heartless. In order to remain accepted by the group, he keeps silent. The majority of the crowd can then claim consensus that there is police brutality. They come out for another protest, this time against police brutality and murder. (It is easy to come up with a similar story for the blue camp.)

Hence, a biased narrative can be "socially" internalised if a manipulator knows how to play the game. It is well known that repeated exposures to an unfamiliar piece of information can increase perceived truthfulness if the piece is not stated as false. One can repeat a lie a thousand times to firm up a group belief. A picture out of context achieves point (i) as in the previous paragraph. Social media achieves point (ii), it is a great facilitator. Human beings' confirmation bias will take over, and each contributes bits and pieces of partial evidence to a firmed up group-wide belief. Note here that the Yellow campers have an advantage, many are youth in school or not yet in employment to make a living. They have time. As previously mentioned, there is also the Dunning-Krueger effect. Pseudo experts vociferously and powerfully lend false credibility to the crowd, thus achieving point (iii). A few rallies, perhaps with some paid participation at first, will generate point (iv). A strong narrative is now formed, confirmed, and accepted by a significant crowd. All of these feels like mass hypnosis, and it is!

Blame narratives and conspiracy theory in Hong Kong

Accountability-light opposition politics has a natural connection with the blame narrative. In the absence of a strong ecology to establish accountability — holding politicians responsible for what they advocate — politicians can get away without taking responsibility for the outcomes their policies create. Yet, they still have to explain unpleasant policy consequences. The natural choice is to blame others. Donald Trump clearly illustrates how a politician tends not to take responsibility and shifts blame to anyone available, from the previous President to the Democrats' impeachment to China.

Blame narrative is often built on a conspiracy theory. Trump has suggested that the US's extraordinary high Covid-19 infection and death rates are the result of a Chinese conspiracy. Building a conspiracy theory to shift blame happens in Hong Kong too. Chapter 4 shows that Hong Kong's younger generation's economic plight is multi-faceted and is due to the combination of multiple confounding factors. The younger generation has a hard time making sense of this complicated world and little patience for boring, detailed explanations. They are susceptible to a blame narrative that gives them a conspiracy: a context and an identifiable "evil" enemy who wants to deny them the "bright" future they deserve.

A blame narrative is conveniently born. As Chapter 3 explained, the Opposition is a coalition with an anti-CPC attitude stemming from the 1989 Tiananmen crackdown. They probably genuinely harbour a sincere desire to establish in Hong Kong a political system free of the control of the party that ordered the crackdown. That is, they want Hong Kong to be "two systems" but not necessarily "one country" under the CPC ruled China. China's CPC is thus the obstacle to their goals, it becomes the evil player in their blame narrative. They may have been trapped in crowd hypnosis as described in the previous sub-section: China's CPC is evil, objecting to it is righteous, and it is not necessary to critically evaluate whether using their position of influence, i.e., as policymakers, to pursue the goal is appropriate. The Opposition camp has already expanded to include retired politicians, school teachers, or academics, labour union organisers, and religious leaders, as described in the previous sub-section. A presumption is made that what they pursue is good for Hong Kong. The larger Opposition camp duly sells the narrative to Hong Kong's youths.

The marketing of this narrative has been successful, as many young people in Hong Kong have fallen victim to confirmation bias. The following is a somewhat dramatised and possibly over generalised description to illustrate my point. *Many Hong Kong youth have internalized that CPC is the evil force behind their current economic plight and uncertain future. There are corroborative casual observations to build their confirmation bias. As they grew up, they were accustomed to degrading treatment of poorer Mainland Chinese immigrants whom they thought were in Hong Kong to greedily grab resources. When these immigrants competed for low wage jobs, they were deemed as under-qualified workers who caused the suffering of the lower-income class. They might have collected first-hand casual observations on misbehaviour by some Chinese tourists. They learned from the mass media and teachers about the CPC's Tiananmen Crackdown and cover-up, China's pollution and corruption problems, the migrant workers' challenging lives, and the "illegally abducted booksellers in Hong Kong by Chinese secret police" (unproven, as explained in Chapter 6), and so on. Later, when more Mainland Chinese came to Hong Kong, thus bidding up housing costs, Hong Kong youth viewed them suspiciously, questioning how they got their wealth. When Mainland Chinese successfully claimed plum jobs in the financial district, Hong Kong youth viewed them as controlling repressors. Year after year, they participated in the rallies described in Chapter 5 and thus were socialised to be anti-China, anti-Chinese, and anti-CPC. Instead of seeing the dynamic path in China's development — the dramatic social, economic, and political changes in China — the younger generation uses these snap-shots to exercise confirmation bias; they now are firm believers of the blame narrative promoted by the Opposition and the CHRF (see Chapter 6). They are the die-hard protesters. (And they turn a deaf ear to less biased and less over-generalising perspectives.)*

Conclusion

In conclusion, we cannot help but lament that accountability-light opposition combined with blame narrative is poisonous. There is a list of grave concerns.

Our first concern is that a blame narrative keeps people from self-reflection and does not induce a positive search for progress. Blame narrative, by nature, is built on not accepting self-responsibility. Thus, the Opposition is not taking responsibility for contributing to Hong Kong's high housing cost, hollowing out in the middle, and declining competitiveness. The younger generation is not taking responsibility for failing to understand China, learn Mandarin, and generally be better prepared for competition. Such needs become corroborative evidence of China's repression. (On the contrary, their parents during the colonial era strived hard to understand the British and to learn to speak and write in fluent English.)

The second concern is that a blame narrative does not induce a society to make holistic efforts to seek better social arrangements and public policies to correct society-wide problems. Thus, Hong Kong has been too busily dealing with passing or not passing the national security law (Basic Law, Article 23), stopping patriotic education, seeking universal suffrage, etc., (not to undermine the political meaning of these issues), instead of using the social and political energy to fix its housing problem, income inequality, shrinkage of job opportunities, decline in the quality of education, and other pressing issues.

The third concern is that a blame narrative is divisive. I do not think we need to elaborate further. The 2019–20 unrest speaks for itself. Let us not rub more salt into the wound.

In fact, a blame narrative generates not just divisiveness. It blinds the crowd, and makes people uncritical of the narrative. It leads to the building up of hatred. Unfortunately, we have seen too much of that in Hong Kong. The younger generation internalises almost blindly the storyline that the CPC is evil, and living under the CPC's ruling is miserable and detestable. Some would rather commit suicide if the CPC cannot be toppled; there were in fact such suicides. Some risk everything to revolt against the CPC. The belief is almost like a hate religion — they would even kill for their belief.

We can see this happening not just in Hong Kong. The US has lots of internal problems: income equality, huge medical expenses and age-ing, racial and class divides, educational decline in the inner cities, etc. It will take pages to detail the list of grievances. These problems are driven by America's poor internal policies, under-performing education system, and deficiency in its political structure. The government has to tackle them. Instead of fixing its problems, the country surprisingly elected Donald Trump who has been promoting nativism and protec-tionism. Its administration ruthlessly uses blame narratives and bully-ing tactics internationally while simultaneously deflecting accountabi-lity and responsibility.

Human beings have to break this poisonous chain running from accountability-light politics to blame narrative to blind, negative, divisive and destructive mass emotions. Unfortunately, at least in the case of Hong Kong, correcting the blame narrative will be an uphill challenge because a whole generation may have already internalised a counter-productive blame narrative.

Chapter 8

The Youth: Their Identity and Education, the Government's Failure

Hong Kong's 2019–2020 unrest has primarily been fronted by a group of young people. They have been the key participants in this movement: posting on social media, rallying peacefully, occupying two campuses, and launching outrageous riots. Among the ~9,000 arrested, 40% are younger than 21, and some are as young as 12. While we do not yet have reliable survey data, it would be reasonable to assume that a very significant portion of the younger generation has a sympathetic attitude.

Their actions may be due to their dissatisfaction with the economic outlook of their future. However, the irony is that these actions further damage their future economic opportunities. While the warmth of brotherhood and sisterhood during the protests may sustain their mood and energy, they have to come to a moment of awakening one day. They may be acting impulsively, but we should not assume that. There are non-economic elements that drive their actions.

The year-long period of confrontation and violence is likely to result in psychological trauma that will leave these youths with deep scars and a distorted view of life. For those who actively participated in the movement, they will find out that they cannot change political reality. For the youth who are bystanders, they will find out that they are viewed as less trustworthy, less employable, and they may have to endure a lot of social, economic, and political uncertainty in the near future.

The fanatical and extremely violent type cannot represent these young people. Many of the young participants of the movement are ingenuous and idealistic. We should seek to understand them better and work with them to resolve underlying issues. This would require an earnest systemic effort. We can start by reading what they have written.

In the following section, I describe what I observe from the LIHKG website. Postings by very active participants of the movement dominate the site. Not denying that postings on LIHKG are biased, I believe the observations shed light on the active participants' attitudes and values. These young people have developed in school a very distorted view of history and a very negatively biased impression of China and its government. These young people thus have internal conflicts in their hearts. They know that they are Chinese, but they have an antagonistic attitude towards being Chinese. They dread the idea that China's government rules over Hong Kong. Struggling with their Chinese identity, they adopt a Hong Kong identity built on negative emotions and destructive energy. They pour their negative and destructive energy into the year-long unrest. They sincerely believe that they are freedom fighters.

This chapter explores what causes these young people to lose their identity and what shape their beliefs. There is colossal government failure in Hong Kong. The consequence is that neither Hong Kong's youths nor Hong Kong, as a society itself, has a coherent national identity or concordant beliefs.

The Revealing Nature of LIHKG Posts

LIHKG is one of the protesters' websites that is publicly accessible. Most messages are written in Chinese with a lot of made-up Cantonese words. Some messages are analytical, albeit biased. However, there are also a lot of very angry messages and some very vulgar curses aimed at the CPC, the Chinese, and the anti-protest camp. The posters openly co-strategise to inflict harm on the CPC, China, Hong Kong, and Hong Kong police. There are many "creative" ideas. For example, there are plots on taking "staged" pictures and then sending them to foreign presses and politicians to keep alive the view that there is police brutality in Hong Kong.

There are also suggestions on how to lobby foreign politicians to impose sanctions on Hong Kong and China. Then, there are postings to update that some under prosecution have successfully fled Hong Kong.

Sometimes, these postings reveal their mindset. For example, a group of protesters was taped brutally beating up a lawyer in the anti-protest camp multiple times on May 27th, 2020 while their accomplices opened umbrellas to conceal the ongoing actions. Multiple videos were taped by people living in the high-rises above the scene. Immediately after the videos went viral, LIHKG had postings alerting the attackers that they had been caught on tape. The postings also suggested that the attackers should shave their hair and throw away their clothes to reduce their chances of being identified. At the same time, there were accompanying postings revealing the injured man's identity, cursing him, and suggesting inflicting harm on his family.

I followed the LIHKG web closely from May 25th to May 29th, 2020. After reading the postings for a few days, I could feel the posters' intensive emotions. Some appear to be eager to take strong actions. However, not every posting is extreme. Not everyone will take actual action on the street. Still, they are firmly on the active participants' side.

Collectively, the postings give readers a glimpse of how these young people think, their emotions, what they advocate, and their values. They harbour very strong negative emotions towards China, the Chinese government, the Hong Kong government, and the Hong Kong police. Sometimes, I feel compelled to use the word hatred to describe their emotions because of the vast amount of destructive energy within them. They are capable of doing anything to challengers of their negative emotions and obstacles to their destructive desire to damage China, its government, and pro-China elements in Hong Kong. There is a blatant disrespect of normal human values; but they are proud of what they are advocating. The website's postings show that they claim they are getting positive reinforcement from foreign governments too, particularly the US.

The group behaves like a cult. They are volunteer civilian soldiers bent on inflicting damage on China's CPC, China, and its international image. They are sustaining the unrest in Hong Kong.

The Root Causes of Such Highly Negative Emotions and Destructive Energy

An illustrative post

What is the inner world of these young people, not just the violent ones, but also the civilised supporters? Occasionally, one can find one or two messages in LIHKG that provide a glimpse of information about the inner world of these youth. The following posting on May 25th, 2020 (translated) is illustrative.

> *I was born after 1997. I happily heard that the British government might allow BNO holders to have the right of abode in the UK.*[101] *However, that does not concern me because I was born after the handover anyway. In school, I heard a lot from my teachers that Hong Kong during the British government's time was a good place to live because the neighbours were friendly and there was public housing. The Governor Chris Patten liked HK egg tarts and Princess Diana was pretty.*
>
> *But I was born too late; I had little idea what that good time was like. We have a tough life. We suffered from the 1997 Asian Financial Crisis, SARS, the locusts from the Mainland, the invasion of the Mainland tourists. Sadly, the government eliminated the colonial past, which killed the local culture.*
>
> *There was the umbrella movement in 2014, and the Fishball revolution in 2016* (Chapter 5 describes these events). *Then the anti-extradition bill movement, the "CPC Wuhan Virus," and now the movement of the National Security Law and National Anthem bill. I do not know if there would be an independence revolution, but we shall be cannon fodders.*

---

[101] The British government was concerned that after the 1997 handover, some Hong Kong residents would claim British residential rights. Thus, the UK passed a law known as the "Hong Kong Act 1985". The Act stipulates that British Dependent Territories citizenship cannot be retained or acquired on or after the relevant date by virtue of a connection with Hong Kong. However, persons who are citizens of British Dependent Territories by virtue of any such connection may acquire a new form of British nationality known as British Nationals (Overseas) before July 1st, 1997 (or before the end of 1997 if born in that year before the relevant date). A BNO holder is subject to UK immigration controls and does not have the automatic right to live or work in the UK, and is also not considered a UK national by the European Union (EU).

I always thought I am Chinese, but I am actually a Hong Konger. Hong Kongers are anti-CPC, which is a globally held value, we live for freedoms.

Hong Kong is unique. It was colonised by the British. It was occupied by the Japanese. We do understand; Japan had a famine, and it had to invade Hong Kong to grab food.

The CPC had launched massacres, its Great Famine (1959–61), People's Communes, and the Cultural Revolution forced many Chinese to flee to Hong Kong. The labourers and brains propelled Hong Kong's growth.

However, the Tiananmen Square Massacre took place; the CPC covered up and even rewrote that part of history. I cannot accept such a brutal and heartless political party to rule over China and Hong Kong. I am devoting all I have to Hong Kong. This is our home. Out the CPC, glory to Hong Kong. Some may migrate out, but they are still Hong Kongers.

Misleading teaching, mass media, political propaganda, and socialisation

There can be multiple interpretations of the above. Some may feel that this is a heartfelt statement by a freedom fighter revolting against an evil dictator. Nevertheless, let us dig deeper. There are a lot of biases. We expect that in social media postings. Still, biases can be revealing, let us examine them.

First, the romanticised account of the British colonial period in the first paragraph is not factual. Hong Kong had a higher crime rate in the 60's and 70's than in the two decades after 2000. Public housing projects were hotbeds for gangs, and many young people were forced to join them for "protection." (This is why Hong Kong has many old gangster movies.) Chapter 5 also documents that Hong Kong had a more severe public housing shortage before 1997 than after; see, also Chapter 4 Figure 5. Indeed, in the 60's and 70's, Hong Kong faced many challenges like corruption, traffic jams, poor urban hygiene, amongst others. Hong Kong's economy made rapid progress in the 1990s; it benefitted substantially from the positive spillovers from China's growth after its economic reforms. Furthermore, after the handover, the phenomenal development continued despite the Asian

Financial Crisis and the SARS epidemic. The sub-section in Chapter 4 titled *A Glorious Record but Incoherent Policies* uses some simple statistics to illustrate this point.

The poster said he/she acquired his/her view about Hong Kong during the British government time from his/her teachers. The biased view could stem from the teachers' selective memory, or incomplete knowledge, or conscious efforts to downplay Hong Kong's achievements after 1997.

Two features in the second paragraph stand out: (i) an insulting statement about Mainland tourists, and (ii) the statement that the Hong Kong government tried to eliminate Hong Kong's colonial heritage and local culture.

The first one is the selling point of anti-China mass media, like the Apple Daily newspaper. After the 2003 SARS epidemic, the Chinese government allowed Mainland Chinese to visit Hong Kong without a visa to promote tourism to stimulate Hong Kong's weak economy. That attracted duty arbitrageurs because Hong Kong is a free port with no sales taxes, while China has high tariffs. Therefore, many "Mainland tourists" were hired hands of duty arbitrageurs and some were Hong Kong gangsters. These hired tourists crossed the border often, sometimes multiple times a day. Hong Kong residents complained that they disrupted orderly shopping. Anti-China mass media loudly reported the inconveniences and called Chinese visitors insulting names. Nevertheless, the problem stemmed from the Hong Kong government's failure to deal with the duty arbitrageurs effectively. (Perhaps some shops in the New Territories where these duty arbitrageurs frequented welcomed the business.) In any case, Hong Kongers' reactions to the inconvenience and some newspapers' exaggerated and biased reporting fed into each other to form a negative attitude.

The accusation that the Hong Kong government did not preserve the colonial heritage and local culture is unfounded. After the handover, the Hong Kong government had to replace the symbol on public post-boxes from a "crown," which represents the British Monarchy, to the "bauhinia flower," which represents the new Hong Kong. This is akin to a corporation changing its letterhead after it has changed its name. The change has nothing to do with eliminating Hong Kong's colonial heritage. However, some in the Opposition camp complained that was an attempt to bury HK's colonial past. Separately, as Hong Kong grew, the government had to move the Queen's Pier in the Central District to build roads as well as to develop shopping areas. (The whole plan included moving the pier to allow military ships to reach the harbour, which had been a practice since the colonial period.) These legitimate efforts in urban planning were distorted by the Opposition camp to be anti-local. The hidden motive was to obstruct the implementation of the previously granted PLA's access to the harbour.

To activate localism, the political faction conveniently ignored the Hong Kong government's substantial spending on preserving Hong Kong's local heritage, including in the arts and culture. The Hong Kong government launched heritage revitalisation schemes, with batches of projects involving 19 historic buildings. It built museums. It even invested in preserving Cantonese opera.[102] By no means has the Hong Kong government met all preservation desires; however, it has done a lot more than the colonial government. Still, the Opposition uses the allegation that the Executive Branch government is erasing local identity to hinder the Executive Branch's work plans and policies and to stir up nativism. For example, as Chapter 5 describes, the Hong Kong Indigenous group, which promotes Hong Kong independence, alleged the patrolling of road-side hawkers on the second day of Lunar New Year as an act of suppressing local identity. The group used that as an excuse to launch a riot in Mong Kok on February 9th, 2016. (Complaints by the residents necessitated the patrol. The affected hawkers were not involved in the riot. Instead, they complained that the stirring up of a riot shut down their business opportunity.)

The deduction from the first two paragraphs in the posting is that the writer has a very distorted view of history favourable to a

---

[102] See LCQ19: Preservation and development of Cantonese opera October 21st, 2009 https://www.info.gov.hk/gia/general/200910/21/P200910210222.htm and BBC, "How Hong Kong preserves its heritage through the smart use of old buildings," http://www.bbc.com/storyworks/capital/city-of-inspiration/heritage.

pre-handover Hong Kong. Teachers, Opposition politicians, and collaborating mass media are selling incomplete information, biased stories, and even non-existent government policies to develop a negative narrative about the Hong Kong government and China. These efforts are ongoing.

The fifth paragraph, which starts with "Hong Kong is unique," reflects very biased accounts of history. The post writer was taught an ultra-revisionist history. The Japanese invasion somehow was billed as understandable because the invaders needed food! That was blatantly incorrect, considering the atrocities and hardships that characterised the Japanese Occupation, evident from the historical artefacts such as those in a recent HKUST Library exhibition.[103] Simply put, Japan was not innocent in WWII. Recently, a group of Hong Kong parents protested that some teachers were teaching distorted history to their young children. Because of the pandemic, classes were conducted via the internet. So parents had the opportunity to access materials that were being taught. They were horrified to learn that their children were taught that the Opium war was launched by the British to ban opium in China and to liberalise the Chinese from opium addiction.[104] (Footnote 6 in Chapter 2 reports the correct historical records.)

These distorted school teachings may explain the 180-degree change in opinion about Chinese people (paragraph 6 vs paragraph 2): Chinese

---

[103] Hong Kong University of Science and Technology Library Exhibition " Three Years and Eight Months: Hong Kong during the Japanese Occupation," October 4th, 2018–31st March 2019, https://library.ust.hk/exhibitions/japanese-occupation/?page=Intro. The Introduction to this exhibition begins: "December 1941 to August 1945 was the darkest period of Hong Kong's history in World War II. During the 'Three years and eight months' under the Japanese Imperial Army's occupation, Hong Kong suffered from the ravages of war, with fear and helplessness permeating citizens' everyday lives."

[104] South China Morning Post, "Hong Kong teacher's history lesson on first opium war 'obviously untrue and unacceptable', says Education Bureau, Teacher from Ho Lap Primary School told pupils first conflict in 1840 started because Britain 'wanted to attack China in an attempt to ban smoking'. School principal apologises and government says it will investigate if teacher is guilty of professional misconduct," April 30th, 2020, https://www.scmp.com/news/hong-kong/education/article/3082292/hong-kong-teachers-history-lesson-first-opium-war.

immigrants before 1997 were recognised as contributing to Hong Kong while the later ones were called insulting names.

The third paragraph in the post reveals the psychological imprint left on the writer in the series of anti-China protests over the past six years (2014–2019) and the 2016 Mong Kok Fishball Riot which was orchestrated by the Opposition to promote nativism (i.e., Hong Kong first). If the post writer is twenty years old in 2020, he or she would have been 14 years old at the start of protests, a very innocent age especially vulnerable to biased indoctrination. It is no surprise that this impressionable young mind would have been influenced by the protests and thus socialised to have a negative attitude towards China and the HK government.

There is a one-sided recollection of the CPC's bad mistakes (paragraph 7) as well as a very one-sided view (paragraph 4) that the world is uniformly anti-CPC, billed as the value of people who love freedoms. Let us ask some questions. Where does this young person get his/her reference points about freedoms? Does he or she not have enough freedoms? Does he or she already possess the desired freedoms but believe that protests are needed to preserve them? What freedoms does this youth worry about losing? Why or why should it not be granted? Not possessing a specific type of freedom cannot be equated to lacking freedoms in general. Is there a leap in logic about the CPC not giving people rights and freedoms?

At the end, the indoctrination effect is clear. There is the logically unsound but morally appealing statement about Hong Kongers wanting and living for freedoms, but the CPC is denying people freedoms, and thus everyone is anti-CPC. In the end, he or she justifies the willingness to be cannon fodder in this movement.

Incomplete information and lack of closure

At the risk of over inferencing, I posit that the message suggests the author has not paid attention to the positive things that China has experienced, especially after the reforms. Also, he or she does not seem to give any weight to changes in the CPC's actions, including the reforms, the abandoning of People Communes, the improvement in public administration, and so on. While the CPC has not openly condemned the terrible past economic policies and political struggles, their actions show that they are correcting from their mistakes. While the CPC at the time whitewashed the Tiananmen Square crackdown and hid that part of history from students, the CPC of recent years has made changes in economic and public policies to drive inclusive growth and to protect the environment.

All societies make mistakes. If we focused only on the negative parts in the history of the United States — slavery, discriminatory treatment of immigrants, corruption, cronyism, non-democratic treatment of minorities, including blacks and women[105] — and did not appreciate the progress it has made over time, we would mistakenly see it as a terrible country dictated by self-serving wealthy power-brokers. The US has continued to make terrible mistakes that violate human rights and freedoms. For example, "The Tuskegee Timeline," reported by the US Centre for Disease Control and Prevention, details the inhuman treatment given to black experimental medical subjects — these subjects were essentially denied their basic human rights. The research was on how syphilis affects health. However, even after penicillin, an effective treatment medicine, was found, the subjects with syphilis were not informed nor treated with it. Many appreciate that President Clinton subsequently apologised for this ugly mistake on behalf of the nation in 1996.[106] The US every now and then reflects upon its mistakes and makes good progress. We should appreciate that. China has done a bit of the same too. (However, the CPC rarely openly admits its mistakes.) Progresses in history often take time and we should be patient.

A few critically important points emerge regarding containing politicised narrative. First, one cannot make a sound and fair judgment without complete information, or at the minimum, balanced information. We also need to be aware that emotions can blindfold objectivity. Second, admitting past mistakes is essential. Government leaders and

---

[105] The US did not grant voting rights to women until 1920. Blacks could not vote until 1965.
[106] See https://www.cdc.gov/tuskegee/timeline.htm.

political parties alike have to apologise for mistakes to bring closure, and to facilitate healing and progressive forward movements. China's CPC should try. (It formally apologised for the mistake in reprimanding Dr. Li Wenliang in Wuhan for sharing alarming information about a potential SARS-like epidemic in Wuhan. It also offered Dr. Li an honorable decoration.[107]) Third, complete and balanced information does not come naturally. It takes conscious and holistic societal effort to provide as balanced and complete information as possible and to train people to conduct triangulation of information. Fourth, a blame narrative, developed for political purpose, is often based on manipulating information to connect a person's experiences so as to arouse emotions.

Ugly politics poisons young minds

Depressingly, many young people, hopefully not all, in Hong Kong are influenced by a blame narrative (which some have internalised) because of concerted efforts from the Opposition coalition as mentioned in Chapter 3: they are teachers, politicians, mass media reporters and editors, and many activists in the CHRF. The young people in the Yellow camp have teachers who feed them with biased perspectives and historical accounts unfavourable to China's CPC. Politicians in the Opposition Coalition, retired or not, feed them with anti-China narratives while their supportive activists organise anti-government and anti-China rallies. The mass media reinforces the bias and provides misleading news while pseudo-experts feed them with pretentious expert advice. These are potent one-two-three punches. Bombarded by biased information and anecdotes, many in the younger generations allow confirmation bias to support their buy-in of the negative narrative further. Over the years, the anti-China and anti-government rallies socialise them to develop a cult-like anti-China and anti-CPC attitude. These young people now believe that they are a part of a global value of being anti-CPC and are bravely fighting for freedoms and democracy at all costs.

---

[107] Some question if these are merely political gestures. See https://www.scmp.com/news/china/society/article/3075984/coronavirus-wuhan-local-police-blamed-mishandling-case-whistle.

One cannot help but lament that politics is dirty. It can be a massive deception exercise to generate very biased perspective with a logically unfounded foundation. People are misled, their passion is spent on causes they believe are worthy, but which in fact are inappropriate. Suffice to say this does not bode well for Hong Kong; it is in serious trouble. A very significant portion of the younger generation has fallen victim to dirty politics. Many have internalised the narrative that China, or maybe just the CPC, is vicious and they do not want to be governed by the CPC, or a government that represents CPC. A portion of them find it righteous to resort to violence to revolt against the CPC. They are capable of damaging anything in their way, using any means, including the violation of well-established human values like honesty and non-violence. They are the foot-soldiers in the unrest.

Identity Loss and Government Failure

The writer of the LIHKG post reveals a sense of loss in identity. Adopting the blame narrative has caused this youth to abandon the Chinese identity conferred by birth. The person has to instead adopt a vague Hong Kong identity. This and other parts in the message vividly showcase the Hong Kong government's failure.

Hong Kong, according to the Basic Law, is an inalienable part of China, its government is directly under Beijing's central government, and China has the option to let the Basic Law expire in 2047. Indeed, the Basic Law requires that the Chief Executive, cabinet members, and all Legislative Council members swear to uphold the Basic Law and allegiance of the HKSAR of the PRC. That means the Executive Branch and the Legislative Council have the responsibility to shepherd Hong Kong in this re-integration journey, with 2047 as a pre-marked landmark decision year. Out of 7.4 million people in HK, 35.5% are between 40 and 11 and 9.7% are younger than 10. These people do not have the same Chinese identity as the remaining older generation. To reintegrate Hong Kong into China, developing in the youth a national identity is a necessary condition.

China's government must be disheartened to see that the proportion of Hong Kongers who identify themselves as Chinese has been on the decline since 2003. The number has dropped to below 20%, according to a survey result; I hasten to add that this survey methodology has not been scrutinised.[108] Still, it is a piece of evidence that the coalition of Opposition — politicians, teachers, mass media, CHRF activists — has succeeded in its concerted effort to build a biased and negative narrative against China, as just explained. The efforts probably started even before 1997. The decline in Hong Kong's young people's Chinese identity feeds the unrest.

This means that the Hong Kong government has collectively failed in its re-integration assignment. The assignment would naturally include the building of national identity in Hong Kong, the fostering of a mutual understanding between Hong Kong and the Mainland in each other's social, cultural, economic, and political landscapes. Hong Kong's government leaders may understand the need for a holistic and coherent long-term plan. However, by nature of their training and the influence of tycoons, they have focused predominantly on economics and free-market principles. They bragged about growth in per capita GDP and stock market performance. Indeed, the rich have become richer. However, the government's scorecard in other aspects is underwhelming.

The Hong Kong government gives observers the impression that they are severely under-trained. By nature of their training, past civil servants are overly focused on following procedures and avoiding blame. They like to mention the "Lion Rock Spirit," which is understood to mean "perseverance and solidarity" as representative of Hong Kong's core value. However, what Hong Kong needs is a direction, a road map, and milestones in its long and challenging post-1997 journey. The government does not speak often enough about facts, differentiate untruths from facts, and explain what is right and wrong for society. It is too wary of taking a stance against populism. Instead, it has

---

[108] See The Economist, "Almost nobody in Hong Kong under 30 identifies as 'Chinese' — The territory's residents increasingly see themselves as distinct from mainlanders," August 26th, 2019, https://www.economist.com/graphic-detail/2019/08/26/almost-nobody-in-hong-kong-under-30-identifies-as-chinese. The article reports a survey result by the HK Public Research Institute. We do not know how credible the survey's methodology is. Still, the trend is similar across all age brackets and deserves attention.

been reactive, too reactive, to the popular press. Thus, the government yields to the Opposition whenever there is a rally or protest. The right things are not done because the feebly-led government tries to do only what is "considered right".

Hong Kong's Executive Branch and its supporting politicians do not connect with people, despite many big warning signs like the umbrella movement in 2014 and the Fishball riot in 2016. The lack of communication and appropriate reactions in dealing with the year-long unrest cements this sense of out of touch, and is worse than expected. Indeed, for decades it let the Opposition drag its nose around. As a result, the Hong Kong government has collectively failed to offer a constructive and exciting vision and mission to Hong Kongers in Hong Kong's historical journey. Along the way, the Executive Branch's very poor leadership has inadvertently allowed others to damage Hong Kong's identity.

The greatest failure may lie in Hong Kong's education system, which underwent a reform in 2009. No state can afford to fail in education. There have been many discussions about Hong Kong's education system failing to build for the students a healthy national identity and values.[109]

National identity is the recognition of communities as a cohesive whole, as represented by distinctive traditions, culture, and language. In recent months, there have been vociferous complaints about Hong Kong's education system which points to many shortcomings. However, before I turn to them I would confess that I have not con-ducted research on education. The followings are collated impressions and anecdotes. Detailed research is needed. I would welcome criticism and correction. Still, I hope to draw attention to the following.

(i) During the colonial period, both Chinese Literature and History were core subjects in school. Generations of Hong Kongers learnt

---

[109] I have benefited substantially from conversations with Dr. Aline Wong, who was born in Hong Kong and was Singapore's Senior Minister of State focusing on education before she retired from politics in 2001. Her insights help me to formulate the rest of this sub-section. All errors are my responsibility.

about Chinese culture and national values through these two sub-jects. In 2009, they became only electives in the Hong Kong Diploma of Secondary Education Exam (HKDSE). As a result, few take the courses (less than 7,500 out of a possible 28,000 candidates).

(ii) The Ministry of Education does not recognise the importance of teaching Mandarin. Divided spoken languages mean divided iden-tities. During the colonial period, learning English was mandatory and some schools conducted all classes in English. It is inexplicable why Hong Kong is lukewarm in teaching Mandarin. Language is a critically important component of a national identity!

(iii) National identity cannot be forced but the Ministry took a poor step by introducing a national education course in the school curriculum, which eventually backfired. The "China Model National Conditions Teaching Manual" was published by the National Education Services Centre under government funding, and described the CPC as an "advanced, selfless and united ruling group." Without passing judgment on CPC, I would submit that such hard-selling unsurprisingly produced resistance; multiple opposition groups were formed including "Scholarism — The Alliance Against Moral & National Education", the "National Education Parents' Concern Group" and the "Civil Alliance Against the National Education". They undertook a protest in 2012. Chief Executive Leung withdrew the national education course. Was this over-reacting? Instead of withdrawing it, why not just improve the content?

(iv) Then, there is the highly controversial "Liberal Studies", formally implemented in 2009 and made a core subject in the Hong Kong Diploma for Secondary Education exam and required for univer-sity entrance.[110] It includes five topics: HK Today, Modern China, Globalisation, Public Health and Energy, Technology and the Environment. There are no set texts (as indeed it is very difficult to set textbooks on current affairs which are rapidly changing all

---

[110] I benefited substantially from Mrs. Aline Wong's insights on this subject matter and broadly on education.

the time). Individual schools and teachers can set their curriculum and teaching materials. The problem is that most teachers are not equipped to prepare their own curriculum and texts. Hence, there are anecdotal reports of teachers resorting to "cutting and pasting" newspaper reports on the mornings of their lessons (as many as 3 hours per week on this subject). What results then is a discussion mostly of HK affairs and often in a biased manner. However, many teachers are not well trained enough to be able to present a truly systematic, evidence-based, balanced view of such issues within a broad understanding of HK's, China's, or the global (developed and developing world) context. The questions in the compulsory public examination component (20% in-school assessment) often over-emphasise current affairs and governance in Hong Kong. The questions on China and world health and environmental problems are skewed towards topics of pollution, epidemic controls, corruption, urban-rural inequality, and so on.

Teenagers go through significant hormonal changes in puberty and these contribute to mood swings and strong emotions like anger. When they receive inadequate guidance on exercising common sense and rational judgment and experience long exposures of negative narratives, there is a high likelihood that they become irate and self-centred. This is especially likely the case given that they have no foundations in history and literature, which have been demoted from being core subjects to electives.

Perhaps, the underlying reason for the colossal failure in Hong Kong's education is that the government inexplicably allowed education to be guided by "market forces". A clear example is the decision by the Ministry of Education to accord teachers complete freedom but little training to teach Liberal Studies.

The saddest part of all these failures is that many in Hong Kong's generation of youth are already lost, and some will keep choosing to do what damages their future further.

Chapter 9

Long- and Short-Term Learning and Solutions

When colonised in 1842, Hong Kong was just a fishing village. The British Empire grew Hong Kong into a significant entrepôt in the China trade. It became the safe harbour for Chinese running away from a troubled China from the time of the Taiping Rebellions (1850–1864) to the 1950s and 1970s when the Communist Party of China carried out terrible policies in China. The British government and China's CPC appeared to have reached a compromise in keeping Hong Kong as a British colony, threat-less to China but serving as its window to the world. Chinese living in Hong Kong were likely grateful for the safe harbour and they focused on making a living. Hong Kong thrived economically as a free port. China's economic reforms since 1978 provided many business opportunities for Hong Kong and further elevated its growth. All of these collectively developed Hong Kong into a charming, vibrant, world-class financial centre with per capita GDP ranked among the most developed countries. It was a free, pleasant, and peaceful city.

Re-joining China when China was engaging in economic reforms and rebuilding, Hong Kong had a chance to show leadership. Hong Kong could have showcased the function of its valuable market institutions: a fair court, efficient and effective regulations, and independent monetary authority. Hong Kong could have strived to be a spirited society, within a communist country, with a vibrant market guided by a government that respects the rule of law, property rights, and individualism. Optimists could visualize a rosy development beneficial to Hong Kong, China, and the rest of the world. Hong Kong may be taking a wrong turn now. However, let us not underestimate Hong Kong. It may turn around; the Pearl of the Orient may shine again.

I will conclude this book first by reiterating Hong Kong's journey to the current large scale and long-lasting social unrest. The critical point is that the unrest has turned into a movement. While the movement is founded on real economic grievance caused by inconsistent policies, its orchestration is rooted in decades of blame narrative. Continuous government failure is a contributing factor too. Reality is that a significant portion of the generation that grew up after 1997 is now involved in the movement. The government has to bring them back to the mainstream of Hong Kong. Second, we shall discuss the implied lessons for the Hong Kong government in the long run. Finally, we discuss what the government should do in the short run.

A Difficult and Sad Journey

The year-long 2019-2020 unrest has tarnished Hong Kong's image, damaged its retail and tourist industries, and eliminated job opportunities. The unrest has become so divisive that Hong Kong now appears to be a vortex of cynicism, distrust, and discordance, with even its governability being questionable. It has also become a pawn in games of international geopolitics, e.g., even its cherished free port status is under threat. However, short-run observations often overshoot reality. We must try to maintain our balance in thinking about Hong Kong's future.

The US, Taiwan, and other regions have benefited from the situation in Hong Kong. However, it is idle to speculate about a "master manipulator." Who can so skilfully come up with a destructive plan to harm China, Hong Kong, and its currently "lost" youth? While external factors play a role, Hong Kong's trouble is intimately related to decades of multi-faceted internal mistakes. Chapters 3 to 8 navigate the path of destruction focusing on these internal problems. The points are summarized below.

To be fair, Hong Kong's economy has done well since the handover until recently. It sailed through the challenging 1997 Asian Financial Crisis, the 2003 SARS epidemic, and the 2008 Great Financial Recession. It has become a premier global financial centre, particularly in serving as a conduit between China's corporations and modern finance. Fast-growing China and Hong Kong have a synergistic economic relationship: Hong Kong receives financial and human capital from China while its low value-added activities migrate to the Mainland. Hong Kong's per capita GDP growth (about 260% from 1990 to 2018) is the envy of the world and its life expectancy is the topmost in the world.

However, accompanying these glowing records are many well-known problems: widening incoming inequality, skyrocketing housing costs, a hallowing out of middle-skill jobs, and shrinking upward mobility for the younger generation. These problems affect the younger generations the most and form the core of their economic grievances. However, these grievances are internally created, driven by Hong Kong's inconsistent public policies since the 1997 handover.

Hong Kong started its re-integration with China in 1997. As described in Chapter 4, neither China nor Hong Kong had a road map for this journey — the absorption of a market economy with advanced Western institutions by a socialist country with almost 200 times its population and a backward economic system. The Basic Law is Hong Kong's mini-constitution established in 1990 that would last for 50 years and possibly even beyond. China follows the Basic Law and leaves Hong Kong alone most of the time unless approached by the Hong Kong government. The hope is that China and Hong Kong will continue following the Basic Law and then time will tell.

Hong Kong's government needs to develop a viable long-term policy vision and direction for Hong Kong's journey. The task goes well beyond just maintaining Hong Kong's economic prosperity. Hong Kong has to make economic and social adjustments to intensifying interactions with China at all levels. In my opinion, Hong Kong should develop the aspiration to take a constructive leading role in modernisation of China. None of the above have happened yet, not even remotely.

The reality is more challenging than expected. The Basic Law, which became effective since the handover on July 1 1997, has liberated Hong Kong from a colonial authoritarian system to a system of democratic opposition politics. It empowers a largely elected Legislative Council to provide checks and balances against the Executive Branch. (Previously, Hong Kong had a colonial authoritarian system. Political power was concentrated in the hands of the British appointed governor. He ran the Executive Branch and presided over the Legislative Council.) The Basic Law therefore defines the "one country, two systems" concept in Hong Kong. "One country" means that Hong Kong is an inalienable part of China. "Two systems" refers to that China runs its socialist system in China while Hong Kong implements the new democratic opposition government system defined by the Basic Law. Preserving the "one country, two systems" is to follow the Basic Law.

Democratic opposition politics can lead to prudent policies if there is accountability. Unfortunately, after one and a half centuries of colonialism, Hong Kong does not have the socio-ecological system to hold politicians responsible for the consequences of their political behaviour. The result is accountability light opposition politics. While there are elections, politicians have too much freedom to pursue self-interest.

The Executive Branch, most of the time, focuses on economic issues and practises non-interventionist economic policies. Members in the Legislation Council are divided into two camps: pro-establishment and pro-democracy. The former emphasizes economic development, is supportive of the Executive Branch, and generally pro-CPC. The pro-democracy camp is a part of the Opposition coalition which first took shape after the 1989 Tiananmen Square Crackdown. It wants to establish its own version of democracy in Hong Kong and to mitigate CPC's influence in Hong Kong.

After 1997, Hong Kong's factionalised politics has produced many inconsistent policies that create economic grievances, which lay the foundation of social unrest. For example, while embracing immigration,

Hong Kong fails to develop matching policies like increasing the supply of affordable housing and public medical services. Similarly, while practising free-market principles, Hong Kong allows monopolists to extract rents. The cost of housing has sky-rocketed. At the same time, the Executive Branch has established layers of bureaucracy that make building structures on land a very daunting exercise. The government has an open-door policy for the flows of financial and human capital from the Chinese mainland. However, it has not adequately prepared its youth for the competition, nor has it helped its youth to explore opportunities in the Chinese mainland. It has not even made learning Mandarin, Chinese literature, and History required subjects in secondary school education. The scarily long list of inconsistent policies have harmed the young generation the most.

Pursuing its goal and not having a blue-print, the Opposition promotes a blame narrative — **the Chinese CPC will take away democracy and personal freedoms from Hong Kong**. In its view, to preserve Hong Kong is to say "no" to China, even if that means not following the Basic Law. At the end, the economic interest of the younger generation is under-represented. For those struggling to make enough to pay rent for a shoe-box size room, their human rights and freedoms is about improving their lots in life.

The Opposition's blame narrative, however, sells. As explained in Chapter 7, human beings use narrative to make sense of complicated life experiences, especially if the narrative has a blame element (i.e., all mistakes are not mine) and a tone of conspiracy (someone devilish is harming us). Recipients of the narrative exercise confirmation bias; that is, they seek only corroborating evidence for the narrative. Chapter 6 explains that China is not guilt-free — it offers corroborative evidence for the narrative and its communication is ineffective. Chapters 5 to 8 show that years of rallies since 2003 and a growing network of machinery — Opposition politicians and their special interest affiliates, the local and foreign reporters, teachers with biased opinions, religious leaders, some academics, student unions — socialise many who grew up after 1997 to believe that China's CPC is repressive and will take away Hong Kong's democracy and freedoms. They also succeed in selling to these younger generations the notion that fighting against the CPC is a global value. Chapters 5 and 7 show that the intensive 2019–20 year-long social unrest and blatantly manipulative propaganda have convinced even more of the younger generation to believe in the narrative. The issue on hand now is that they do not want China's CPC to rule over them.

Of course, the truth is a lot more complicated. Certainly, the CPC would not tolerate a direct challenge to its political monopoly; it has more restrictions on criticism of the government than most countries. However, it does not prohibit constructive discussion on how to govern China better. The following questions are worth pondering: What is democracy and freedom truly? How does the CPC run the country? How could the CPC be comprehensively assessed in a balanced manner? These are complicated issues with no one-size-fits-all answers. Trivialisation of these topics into a simple blame narrative is unwise and highly misleading.

The problem is, many people are fooled! (Apologies for the strong word.) Is the blame narrative related to the tilted growth, wealth inequality, the rising cost of living, shrinking opportunities in the middle, and dimming future economic outlook for the less privileged? Is the blame narrative intimately related to the happiness of the majority of ordinary Hong Kongers? How many Hong Kong residents fully understand what freedoms China is and is not taking away? How many indeed want to topple the CPC? The well-being of ordinary Hong Kongers is not well represented in the tug of war between the Opposition, which promotes the narrative, and the pro-establishment camp.

The blame narrative with a tone of conspiracy has disproportionately dominated Hong Kong's political and policy discussion since the 2000s. Pro- vs. anti-China are both equated to preserving Hong Kong, Hong Kong's system, Hong Kongers running Hong Kong, and being faithful to "one country, two systems". The two sides (the Opposition and the pro-establishment) have contradictory definitions for each of these ideals. Cynical debates continue. The pro- vs anti-China policy stances pre-determine judgement and trump logical analyses. Hong Kong's long-term policy needs and direction are ignored. The sacrifices are coherent policies, inclusive growth, and developing a future for the younger generations.

Friedrich von Hayek said in his Nobel lecture (1974) that, "*To act on the belief that we possess the knowledge and the power which enable us to shape the processes of society entirely to our liking, knowledge which in fact we do not possess, is likely to make us do much harm.*"[111] This statement applies to many of the politicians and pseudo-experts in Hong Kong's accountability-light politics — these politicians and pseudo-experts have no true knowledge but just a narrative that has not passed rigorous scrutiny. Yet, they adopt the high moral ground and sell the narrative to Hong Kongers, particularly young people, and many amongst the young generation are now lost in rebellions against the Executive Branch and China. Hong Kong's problem is not social unrest anymore. It is how to work with these young people, better yet, how to bring these souls back into meaningful rational discussions.

The Market, State, and Society

The government has the responsibility to provide remedies and solutions for the current situation. I use the term government to refer collectively to the Executive Branch, the Legislative Council, and various political factions. This section does a stocktake of the long-run lessons.

Conjectures about the future

The current unrest will eventually settle, one way or the other. It is quite likely that Hong Kong would not experience dramatic institutional changes other than that the national security measures will outlaw secessionist and subversive activities as well as foreign interference and

---

[111] Friedrich August von Hayek — Prize Lecture, <https://www.nobelprize.org/prizes/economic-sciences/1974/hayek/lecture/>.

terrorism in the city. Hong Kongers will not lose many freedoms other than that. (Some foreign countries will fight against losing their interference in Hong Kong, much of which is targeted at China. However, their countries have similar laws, and the Basic Law does allow either China or Hong Kong to establish such laws.) Nevertheless, given the experience of the 2019–20 unrest, there will be intensified pressures from China for Hong Kong to be more cooperative with the Mainland government, in line with the interests of China and the CPC (which the US Secretary of State Michael Pompeo explicitly commented is against (his version of) the US's interests).

The path forward for Hong Kong will be complicated. Different groups in society — the rich, the poor, the young, and the old — will have adjustments to make. The dominance of established businesses will not fade. Their dominance may even grow as the unrest and the pandemic have harmed many small and medium-sized companies. Companies from the Chinese mainland will continue to expand in Hong Kong. Foreign businesses headquartered in Hong Kong, and targeting the Chinese mainland market, may move directly into the Chinese mainland because of the local political uncertainty. Also, the mainland practitioners and policymakers have downgraded their opinion of Hong Kong, particularly the quality of the younger workforce. Then, Hong Kong has to deal with that a very significant portion of the younger generation who has adopted the blame narrative against China.

The answer to these daunting challenges is, however, nothing unusual. There is a time-honoured Chinese advice: a harmonious family is prosperous. Hong Kong needs to rebuild multiple factions' mutual acceptance and understanding of one another. It needs to produce inclusive growth from here on. We should have confidence. China cares about Hong Kong's continuous prosperity; it does want the "one country, two systems" as defined by the Basic Law to succeed. Many people in Hong Kong and around the world want to see Hong Kong return to peace, happiness, and prosperity. Historically, under similar conditions, Hong Kong has bounced back amazingly well from the verge of collapse multiple times. (See Chapter 2.)

The charge of the government

Hong Kong's government has to do two things which it should have done before. It should provide balanced and adequate representation of the well-being of various constituents in Hong Kong. It should also cultivate the development of an intelligent community with a common identity.

A modern state comprises the government, market, and society. Advanced economies cannot do without a market. The decision-makers in the market are capitalists. They have decision rights over investment, deployment of capital (including intellectual capital), sourcing, pricing, wages, and employment. Capitalists, first and fore-most, make decisions to benefit themselves. Thus unfettered market behaviour can create pain for the masses.[112] **Whichever way Hong Kong further evolves, the government has to provide a balanced representation for the capitalists and the masses (both the current and future generations) in mediating their concerns, protecting their interests prudently, allowing them options and freedom of choices, overcoming market failures, and generally safeguarding the boundary of acceptable behaviour as well as the rule of law to attain overall efficiency, stability, and fair redistribution. These are the essence of democracy and freedoms; they are not the sole characteristics of a unique system; they should be the desired outcome of any system.**

However, a government is made up of people. People can be self-centred, can make mistakes, and can fall captive to special interest

---

[112] Marx and Engel, concerned about capitalistic abuse of labourers, advocated working-class supremacy: communism in which a benevolent state takes over the market and makes allocation, production, and consumption decisions. Thinkers like Hayek would point out the gross inefficiency of such an arrangement due to a lack of incentives to collect the right information to make and execute decisions in a timely manner. Furthermore, the decision-makers in this setting pursue self-interest too. Their decisions can be devoid of economic reality and can harm the masses, particularly in a strong hierarchy. For example, in such settings, subordinates tend to tell decision-makers what they think decision-makers want to hear instead of what they should hear. In history, forced practices of naïve communism never failed to create economic hardships for many.

groups. Such "captives" make democracy fail. Hong Kong's government has been held captive by multiple groups.

Earlier thinkers like English James Harrington (1611–1677), author of *The Commonwealth of Oceana* (1656) would argue that ownership of property was the source of power and would dominate the government.[113] This kind of capture is well known, e.g., Rajan and Zingales wrote brilliantly and convincingly about "Saving capitalism from capitalists" (2004).[114] Cronyism leads to de facto dictatorship, limiting real freedoms and democracy no matter what voting system a society has. Resources remain in favour of the elites. Hong Kong's economic history suggests that the government in the colonial time was captive to the "Hongs" and "Taipans" and now is excessively friendly to the local tycoons. Hong Kong's wealth distribution remains very skewed.[115]

Hong Kong has an additional but unique problem. The Opposition has held itself captive because it is bonded together by the blame narrative as depicted in the previous section and Chapters 6 and 7. The camp has to continuously find issues to justify the blame narrative that China's CPC is eroding Hong Kong's democracy and freedoms and undermining Hong Kong's system. The blame narrative gives legitimacy to the camp's anti-China policy stances. In other words, ***the Opposition has become a captive to its own blame narrative***. The blaming game also dilutes attention to the Opposition's share of responsibility in developing public policies that damage the future of the younger generations.

---

[113] James Jarrington (1656) *The Commonwealth of Oceana*, printed for Livewell Chapman by "https://en.wikipedia.org/wiki/John_Streater" John Streater; London.

[114] Raghuram Rajan and Luigi Zingales (2004) *Saving Capitalism from the Capitalists*. New York: Crown Business.

[115] A government can also be the capture of opportunistic populists that can lead to economic stagnation. Politicians gear to represent short term special interest to gain immediate support and build a long-term mutual dependence between them and special interest groups. Politicians need the vote of the special interest to stay in office while the special interest gets from politicians short-term help which makes no long-term improvements on their situation. The special interest group may vary in its composition over time. Policies are naturally incoherent over time. The society stagnates.

Still, we really ought not to completely disparage the Opposition. Many the Opposition camp's issues — safeguard against excessive profit-seeking of the super-rich and the preservation of Hong Kong's rule of law and institutions, including the freedoms of expressions and associations (see Article 27, Basic Law) — are real and worthy of attention. For example, it was indeed the arrival of money from wealthy Mainlanders together with developers' profit-seeking behaviour that drove up Hong Kong's housing costs (see Chapter 4). China's flexing of its economic and political muscles can limit Hong Kong's freedoms (see Chapter 6). It is just that the "anti-China" psychology inhibits the Opposition from thinking and working constructively and rationally with others to address these stresses.

The point, however, is that Hong Kong's government has collectively failed to provide a balanced representation of its multi-faceted constituents. Representation builds on accountability. However, representation should not be allowed to develop divisiveness; a society should strive for balanced representation. Accountability and balanced representation are built on a society's strong internal characteristics as in the following.

Common identity

No society is perfectly homogenous; it always has multiple sub-groups. Most policy decisions involve balancing non-uniform current and future gains and costs among different groups for a greater common good. An intelligent society with a common identity can understand policy constraints and trade-offs. With adequate communication, it will prudently accept necessary short-term personal costs for common long-term goods. It can deliberate and choose among alternative policies what is the best for society.

The optimism stems from that while human beings are self-centred, they are also group-oriented. We often are willing to make sacrifices for the group we belong to, like a family member making sacrifices for the family. This could be because there are tangible (e.g., share in family wealth) and intangible values (e.g., the warmth of love) in group membership. We often observe that a group with a well-accepted identity has solidarity, and group members can accommodate individual differences. Hence, a group is stronger the more its members accept the group identity. Thus, all nations are keen to develop and maintain a national identity.

Developing a national identity has always been the responsibility of educational institutions and the government. Most governments work hard to establish a sense of statehood via education. The Chapter 8 illustrates a Hong Kong youth's lamentation of identity loss. The last section of the same chapter argues that Hong Kong's government and its education system have to provide the remedy.

The Ministry of Education has to think hard about how the older generations of Hong Kongers acquired their firm Chinese identity from their education. They were exposed to Chinese literature and history: language, literature, and history are all critically important components of our identity. National identity is built from each student's internalisation of national culture, values, and historical judgement on the right vs. the wrong attitude and behaviour towards one's country. Exposures to the Tang and Song peoms (唐詩宋詞), the four classic novels, namely *Romance of the Three Kingdoms* (三国演議), *Journey to the West* (西遊記), *Water Margin* (水滸傳), and *Dream of the Red Chamber* (紅樓夢), and the writings by ancient Chinese philosophers such as *Analects of Confucius* (論語) by Confucius (孔子) shape our understanding of China and its culture. *Historical Records* (史記)" by Sima Qian (司馬遷) and stories about historical national heroes [e.g., Fan Zhongyan (范仲淹) in the Northern Song Dynasty (北宋), Yue Fei (岳飛) in the Southern Song Dynasty (南宋), and Lin Zexu (林則徐) in the Qing Dynasty (清)] shape our identity and capacity to make judgement between right and wrong. This is how education had inculcated the Chinese national identity into the older generation of Hong Kongers. Their love for China had nothing to do with what any Chinese government had done for them. In fact, most of them who moved to Hong Kong ran away from the Chinese governments.

Now, the work has to be extended to the generations that grew up after 1997. This challenging task is gravely important. Hong Kong needs its youth! I have to confess that I am no expert on this issue. Moreover, this gravely important matter requires earnest crowd-sourcing of wisdom. The work likely involves countering the current indoctrinated biases. One way to overcome this is to allow people to reacquire a comprehensive and balanced perspective of Hong Kong's culture and history and its relationship with China (including its reliance on China as well as its contribution to China's economy). It will also involve reconnecting Hong Kongers (especially the youths) with thousands of years of Chinese culture and history. They also need to be re-exposed to a balanced account of contemporary Chinese history in the past one and a half centuries. The work likely involves the participation of artists and other members in the cultural industries. Very importantly, the job ought to include a universal search for a constructive mission of Hong Kong in the 21st Century, in the context of a still-developing China facing numerous international and external challenges.

An intelligent society

A society is intelligent if the majority of individuals can sieve out biased information, unfounded rumours and fake news, be open to rational debates, and can make an informed judgement on public events and policies and on their short- and long-term implications. In the current era of technological advancement, people process much information via instant messages and smartphones. The spread of unfounded information can be extensive and instantaneous. Individuals tune in to quick readings that are effective on emotional amplification but short on content deliberation. Even established mass media has appeared to pander to the business of emotional amplification (for readership) than for the provision of balanced content. Developing an intelligent society is thus a matter of paramount importance in the modern era. It is also a necessary step in mitigating accountability-light politics.

In an intelligent society, a very significant proportion of its members practise critical thinking, which includes identifying assumptions and logic audits of causal statements as well as their conclusions. An intelligent society embraces serious efforts to seek and reveal facts, diversity in perspectives and opinions across, as well as open discussions and debates. The building and maintenance of an intelligent society requires a collaborative effort on the part of the educational institutions and the government.

Education develops critical thinking and the government cultivates the development of opportunities for intellectual deliberation.

I lived in New York City during the time of September 11th, 2011. The city was in anguish. I asked my son about the related discussions they were having in his high school (Bronx Science High, New York City). He said that in classes they sought rational explanations for the terrorists' attack; they discussed the Middle-East countries' social and economic struggles and sufferings; they also discussed the world's concerns about terrorism. I very much appreciate the education he received. (Certainly, his education experience may well be atypical.) More recently, among postings on Twitter and the videos on YouTube regarding the protests against the unfortunate death of George Floyd in Minneapolis, US (May 29th, 2020) due to police brutality, there are attempts to steer discussions away from emotions and direct towards correcting racism in a calm and prudent manner.

On the contrary, the year-long unrest in Hong Kong showcases its lack of intelligence as a society. Chapter 5 shows how the content of the amendment to the extradition bill was distorted. Then there were the numerous unfounded rumours of police murdering people in the Prince Edward MTR station, throwing murdered bodies into the harbour, and raping a girl in a police station. Somehow, all these unfounded rumours were taken as "facts" and some citizens until recently regularly held vigilance to "commemorate these tragedies". While there are exceptions, most mass media deliver shallow or even biased reports. This is the environment the Hong Kong government has to improve on.

An imperative task is to improve education in Hong Kong. No educators in Hong Kong should feel good about the above observations. Education plays an important role in developing young people's minds. The previous chapter, especially the last section, explains the Hong Kong government's failure in education. It should not, in the name of following the "market principle", let individual schools and teachers decide on how to approach the subject of "liberal studies". It should not let under-trained teachers teach the subject with no textbooks and teaching materials. It should not leave the training of critical thinking to such an under-prepared core course. Any decent educator knows that critical thinking is developed over many years of study and practice across a broad collection of subjects including mathematics, natural science, social science, statistics, and humanities. Over time, students develop their analytical skills (via mathematics, statistics, and logic), cognitive skills (evidence, reasoning, deduction, and inference), and creativity (via arts and mathematics).

A point is worth emphasising — **halt the teaching of judgements.** We should refrain from teaching young minds judgements which are essentially opinions. (Teaching judgement is different from teaching values. For example, we can explain the value of love and care in a class, but we should refrain from telling students that a certain political party loves and cares for people, or is absolutely evil.) Young people are susceptible to premature internalisation of the opinions of authority figures and seniors whom they respect. Taught judgement can thus become indoctrination, that is, judgement without adequate evaluation on the soundness of the judgement. When the teaching of judgement is widespread, society becomes unintelligent.

There are other areas that Hong Kong's government needs to work on. The government should take the lead to improve the quality of mass media content and policy research related to Hong Kong. As Chapter 5 points out, the lack of investigative reporting in Hong Kong is saddening. The government has to invest in improving its education in journalism. Perhaps, Radio Hong Kong should be evaluated based on comprehensiveness and balance in its reporting. The government has to take the lead to cultivate and facilitate the right environment, e.g., by nurturing rational public discussion and responsible reporting, i.e., fact-based reporting, but, of course, not at the expense of freedom of expression. Finally, the government should take the lead in developing research to assist in evidence-based policymaking.

A Short-Run Solution

Re-building an intelligent society with a common identity is the right long-term direction for Hong Kong's government. Hong Kong, however, needs immediate short-term remedies.

Hong Kong's year-long unrest may very well decrease in scale as fatigue sets in. The National Security Law is a deterrence to some. The police may possibly become more effective than before in containing protest activities before they erupt into destructive disturbances of ordinary life. However, the movement is driven by a sizeable portion of the younger generation who grew up after 1997. The movement can continue without stepping into the forbidden zones defined by the National Security Law. Life in Hong Kong will not be normal as compared to pre-unrest days. The discordance will be annoying and damage Hong Kong in multiple ways, including outward migration of human and financial capital, corporation headquarters, and the loss in incentives for indigenous young people to invest in human capital.

That may be too pessimistic. Many still have faith and believe Hong Kong can bounce back like before. Still, it would be useful to search for constructive solutions.

Deterrence will not stop the movement

We need to understand the drivers of the movement. As the quote in Chapter 8 says, the post writer commits "all I have to Hong Kong. This is our home. Out the CPC, glory to Hong Kong". The year-long unrest is fronted by extremists in the younger generation. However, due to the Hong Kong government's poor management and manipulative emotion-arousing social and mass media messaging, many in Hong Kong, especially in the younger generation, have become sympathetic and supportive. The hard drivers of the movement are gaining psychological and emotional energy from these supporting peers.

Other factors are sustaining the movement. The US gains political benefits from sustaining the movement. Its close allies have also shown their support. Taiwan's Democratic Progressive Party gains from the movement too. They all offer these young people encouragement and support. The National Security Law cannot fully stop them. The Opposition politicians in Hong Kong gain benefits from the movement too. They would continue to encourage it.

Even if the government manages to totally eradicate the movement, this large group of disgruntled people will remain a problem for Hong Kong. Furthermore, no government should ever contemplate governing a significant portion of the population that is highly discontent with the government system and their lives.

The tactic of arrest and prosecution is not a real remedy. This tactic can be difficult because Hong Kong's judiciary system is not easily changeable in the short run, and doing so shakes up the foundation of Hong Kong's rule of law as well as affects a basic premise in the Basic Law — Hong Kong retains its independent judiciary. Furthermore, using a stick to stop the behaviour does not change the root cause, which is a large scale dissatisfaction.

Re-engage

The government has to re-engage the group. As Chapters 6 to 8 explain, these young people have adopted and internalised a blame narrative. The young people driving the movement may have no constructive objective. They know that "independence" is not feasible. When push comes to shove, they may not even want independence. However, they want to be heard. If their numbers are low, isolating them may be viable. However, their numbers are not negligible.

Many of them have sincere feelings for Hong Kong, whether they are misled or just foolish. After all, they grew up in Hong Kong, under the current regime. The Executive Branch and the current leaders of society have the responsibility to re-engage them: allow them to have a sense of constructive ownership and responsibility in building Hong Kong's future. The Executive Branch should listen to them, sort out differences, and seek understanding and compromise to move Hong Kong forward, including some sensible governmental reforms. All these have no bearing on the importance of finding facts, identifying unlawful behaviour on all sides, and enforcing laws properly. Indeed, that is the rule of law!

The engagement cannot be done in a manner as representing Beijing. Hong Kongers must run Hong Kong. As explained in this book, the current troubles are driven by Hong Kong's internal problems. The Hong Kong government has the lion's share of responsibility. The Executive Branch, the pro-establishment, and the pro-democracy camp should sit down to reflect on the mistakes they have made. In particular, they should ask whether they have sincerely served the younger generations' interests. Self-reflection and admission of errors are acts of courage, rather than weaknesses.

Move forward

All parties in Hong Kong should take the chance to practice constructive dissatisfaction — to do something positive to change the dissatisfying situation. In life, the worst time is the best time for reconciliation and cooperation. Given the massive suffering, economically, individually, in the family and society, it is time for all parties — politicians in all camps, police, protesters, civilian groups, the mass media, and many more — to ask themselves whether they have, individually or collectively, contributed to the mayhem due to their decisions and behaviour in the past or present, no matter how noble their original motivation might have been. It is time to step back, to stop pointing fingers, and to admit guilt. That would be a major step toward long-term healing and redevelopment.

The government, the market, and society can then work together to discuss and develop a consensus on a revived policy direction for a better future. Thus, the government should take the lead to develop a **"Government-Citizen Partnership Forum for a Better Future"**. Widespread consultation can shape Hong Kong's policy priorities and goals in the next decade. Having such a forum then allows for the development of multiple working groups to identify approaches to fix Hong Kong's economic, social, and political challenges. These potential government-citizen partnerships can include, e.g., developing public housing and affordable housing, assisting the younger generation in lifelong learning and entrepreneurship, creating industrial renewal, enhancing government representativeness, improving government-public communications and relations, redesigning income and inheritance taxes, advancing senior care, enhancing community health care, and so on. The list is long but energising. This government-citizen partnership should be a sustained long-term platform which aims to continue to serve Hong Kong for decades.

Fundamentally, Hong Kongers can re-engineer a new consensus to allow the city to move forward constructively based on inclusive growth and a balanced and rational approach to solve social issues. The participants should all be Hong Kongers and all agree to shield themselves from outside influences; that is, Hong Kongers run Hong Kong. Hong Kong can become a shining example to the world about what an intelligent society with a coherent community spirit can do — be our own rational master who consciously and mindfully chooses to do the right thing. The world will regain respect for Hong Kong.

Let us conclude with a positive thought. Hong Kong can demonstrate that a wise and caring government, a disciplined market, and an informed society with a collective identity can collaborate to develop a positive path for inclusive growth. The situation in Hong Kong is not unique. The world faces disruptive changes due to decades of globalisation and technological progress, aggravated by the need to accommodate the economic growth of populous Asian countries. Wealth and income disparity grows and economic anxiety mounts. These naturally create massive dissatisfaction and fear. Opportunistic politicians adopt blame narratives that harness negative energy from the dissatisfaction to advance aimless destructive actions. Sometimes, they lead to nativism and nasty identity politics. The uncontrollable social media collaborate to fuel emotions that deter rational thinking. It is not the time to judge. It is time to understand and seek positive solutions together. The world can be better. It is my sincere hope that Hong Kong will be able to set a positive example of turning destructive satisfaction into constructive reflection and cooperation for a better and more pleasant future!

Printed in the United States
by Baker & Taylor Publisher Services